TROMSØ TRAVEL GUIDE 2024

Your Gateway To The Northern Lights, 7 days Itinerary For You

Myrna Andrew

No part of this book may be reported in any form or by any electronic or mechanical means including information storage and retrieval systems, without permission in writing from the publisher, except by a reviewer who may quote brief passages in a review. This book is a work of nonfiction. The views and opinions expressed in this book are the author's own and do not necessarily reflect those of the publisher or any other person or organization. The information in this book is provided for educational and informational purposes only. it is not intended as a substitute for professional advice of any kind.

Copyright 2024 © **Myrna Andrew** All rights reserved.

GRATITUDE APPRECIATION

Thank you for considering this book as part of your journey! Your support is incredibly appreciated, and I hope it adds value to your travel experience. Every page was crafted with care to help you make the most of your adventure. If you enjoy it, I'd be grateful if you could leave a review to share your thoughts. Your feedback not only helps improve future editions but also guides others in their travels. Thank you again, and may your journey be filled with unforgettable moments!

TABLE OF CONTENT

TROMSØ TRAVEL GUIDE 2024.................1
Your Gateway To The Northern Lights, 7 days Itinerary For You....................1
GRATITUDE APPRECIATION............... 3
TABLE OF CONTENT................................4
INTRODUCTION....................................... 7
Chapter 1... 19
Getting to Tromsø.................................. 19
   By Air..19
   By Sea..22
   By Land... 25
Chapter 2... 30
Accomodation.. 30
   Luxury hotels...30
   Budget friendly hotels.........................71
   Booking tips and website................. 95
Chapter 3... 102
Must-Visit Attractions........................ 102

Northern Lights..102
Arctic Cathedral..106
Polaria Aquarium..110
Tromsø Kunstforening.....................................114
Tromsø Domkirke..117
Arctic-Alpine Botanic Gardens..................... 120
Tromsø Catholic Church............................... 124
Chapter 4.. 126
Outdoor Activities..128
Hiking and Trekking in Tromsø..................... 128
Dog sledding... 130
Snowmobiling..134
Chapter 5.. 139
Cultural experience..140
Sami Culture and Reindeer Sledding............140
Tromsø International Film Festival................144
Chapter 6.. 148
dining and culinary..148
Local Delicacies.. 150
Best Restaurants in Tromsø........................ 153
Chapter 7.. 158
shopping and souvenir..................................... 158
Local Market..160
Boutique Stores...163
Chapter 8.. 166
Practical information tips..................................166
Currency and Payment in Tromsø............... 168
Language and Communication..................... 173
Safety Tips and Emergency Contacts..........177

5

Steps to Scan The QR code.......................... 183
7 Days itinerary for you................................. 184
Day 1: Arrival and Exploration.......................184
Day 3: Fjord Tour and Dog Sledding.............186
Day 4: Sami Culture and Reindeer Sledding 187
Day 5: Snowmobiling and Tromsø Cable Car..... 188
Day 6: Whale Watching and Arctic-Alpine Botanic Garden... 189
Day 7: Shopping and Souvenirs.................... 190
30 phrases in Tromsø................................... 191
Conclusion.. 194

INTRODUCTION

Steps to Scan the QR code is discussed in chapter 8

Tromsø, often celebrated as the **"Gateway to the Arctic,"** stands as a beacon of northern beauty and adventure. Located in the far north of Norway, this city occupies a unique place on the map, roughly 350 kilometers north of the Arctic Circle. The town's location on Tromsøya, an island surrounded by magnificent fjords and snow-capped mountains, offers a captivating blend of urban life and untamed wilderness. Its geography, rich history, and proximity to the polar region make it one of the most intriguing destinations in the world.

Tromsø's Unique Geographic Setting

Tromsø's most distinct feature is its location on Tromsøya, an island in the Tromsøysundet strait. This narrow stretch of water separates the island from the mainland on the east, while to the west, the vast and rugged island of Kvaløya provides a dramatic backdrop. The city's total area extends beyond Tromsøya to encompass parts of Kvaløya and the mainland, all of which are connected by a series of bridges and tunnels, allowing seamless movement across these natural barriers.

Surrounding Tromsø are the fjords—deep, glacially carved inlets with steep, mountainous sides. The Tromsøysundet strait and the larger Balsfjord in the region serve as crucial waterways that have historically been vital for transportation, trade, and fishing. The towering peaks of the Lyngen Alps, just a short distance from the city, offer a breathtaking view and set the stage for countless outdoor adventures. These natural elements contribute to Tromsø's mystique, as the city feels cradled by nature yet is firmly rooted in modernity.

Tromsøya: The Heart of the City

The majority of Tromsø's urban activity takes place on Tromsøya, a relatively small island just 10 kilometers long and 3 kilometers wide. The island is home to the city center, where traditional wooden houses line the streets, blending old-world charm with modern structures. This fusion of architectural styles reflects the city's growth over the centuries, from a small trading post to a bustling Arctic metropolis. At the heart of Tromsøya lies Lake

Prestvannet, a serene freshwater lake surrounded by lush greenery in the summer and snow-covered paths in the winter. It serves as a natural retreat for locals and visitors alike, offering a peaceful contrast to the lively city center. The lake's proximity to the center of town highlights the way Tromsø seamlessly integrates nature into its urban landscape. The island is also surrounded by water, with the Tromsøysundet strait to the east, separating it from the mainland, and the fjord to the west leading toward Kvaløya. This watery environment is intrinsic to the daily life of Tromsø's residents, who have long depended on the sea for fishing, transport, and recreation.

Kvaløya: Nature's Frontier

Just to the west of Tromsøya lies Kvaløya, one of Norway's largest islands. The name Kvaløya translates to "Whale Island," an homage to the majestic creatures that can often be spotted in the surrounding waters. Kvaløya is a rugged, mountainous island characterized by its wild, untamed beauty. This island, with its towering peaks and deep fjords, offers a stark contrast to the more urbanized Tromsøya. Its highest peak, Store Blåmann, reaches an impressive 1,044 meters and is a popular destination for hikers and adventurers. The island is sparsely populated, with small fishing villages dotted along its coastlines, but it is a paradise for nature lovers. The landscape of Kvaløya offers a multitude of activities, including hiking, fishing, skiing, and wildlife viewing. In winter, Kvaløya becomes a wonderland for snow sports enthusiasts, while in summer, the Midnight Sun casts a golden glow over the island, creating long days perfect for outdoor exploration.

The fjords surrounding Kvaløya, including the famous Kaldfjord and Ersfjord, are known for their serene beauty. These fjords are a favorite among kayakers and boaters, who often venture into the calm waters to take in the majestic scenery and observe the local wildlife, including seals and seabirds. Whale watching is particularly popular here during the winter months when orcas and humpback whales migrate to the region to feast on herring.

The Mainland: A Gateway to the Lyngen Alps
To the east of Tromsøya lies the mainland, where the city extends across a mountainous terrain. This area serves as the gateway to some of Norway's most dramatic natural landscapes, including the Lyngen Alps, a range of jagged, glacier-topped peaks that rise sharply from the fjords below. The Lyngen Alps are renowned for their beauty and are a haven for mountaineers and backcountry skiers, offering some of the most challenging and rewarding terrain in Scandinavia. The mainland area is also home to the Tromsdalen Valley, a picturesque valley that stretches from the city center to the foothills of the surrounding mountains. This valley is a popular starting point for many hiking and cross-country skiing routes, including the trail to Tromsdalstinden, a prominent peak that offers panoramic views of the city and its surroundings. One of the most notable landmarks on the mainland

is the Arctic Cathedral, a striking piece of modern architecture that stands at the entrance to Tromsdalen. Its sharp, angular design is said to resemble icebergs or the steep mountains that rise from the fjords, and it serves as a symbol of Tromsø's connection to the Arctic.

Tromsø's Polar Connection

One of the most intriguing aspects of Tromsø's geography is its proximity to the North Pole. Located well above the Arctic Circle, the city experiences extreme variations in daylight throughout the year. From late May to late July, the sun never sets, bathing the city in the Midnight Sun, a phenomenon that provides 24-hour daylight. This period is marked by long, bright summer days, where locals and visitors alike take advantage of the endless sunlight to enjoy outdoor activities late into the night. Conversely, from late November to mid-January, Tromsø experiences the Polar Night, a period when the sun does not rise above the horizon. However, the darkness is far from complete, as the sky is often illuminated by a twilight-like glow during the day, and at night, the Northern Lights (Aurora Borealis) dance across the sky. Tromsø's location makes it one of the best places in the world to witness this natural light show, with the Northern Lights often visible on clear nights from September to April. This unique relationship with the sun and the polar environment has shaped the way of life in Tromsø. During the long summer days, the city buzzes with activity, as festivals, outdoor concerts, and midnight hikes fill the calendar. In winter, the focus shifts to more introspective activities, such as cozying up in cafes or embarking on winter excursions like dog sledding and snowshoeing.

Strategic Importance and Historical Role

Tromsø's location also lends it strategic importance as a northern outpost. Historically, the city has been a vital center for Arctic exploration. It served as a base for numerous expeditions to the North Pole, including those led by famous explorers such as

Roald Amundsen. Tromsø's ice-free port, even in winter, made it an ideal launching point for ships heading into the Arctic.

The city's strategic location also made it a key site during World War II, as it served as an important naval base for German forces. Tromsø's geography, with its fjords and mountains, provided natural defenses, and the city's proximity to the Arctic shipping lanes was of great importance during the conflict. After the war, Tromsø rebuilt and transformed into the vibrant Arctic capital it is today.

Tromsø's Integration with Nature

What truly sets Tromsø apart is the seamless integration of nature and urban life. While the city offers modern conveniences and a lively cultural scene, nature is never far away. Whether it's the forested trails of Tromsøya, the rugged peaks of Kvaløya, or the fjords and mountains of the mainland, Tromsø's geography offers countless opportunities for outdoor exploration.

In summer, locals and visitors take to the hiking trails, fjords, and islands to soak up the Midnight Sun, while in winter, the snow-covered landscape becomes a playground for winter sports enthusiasts. Tromsø's natural setting also plays a role in its sustainability efforts, as the city actively promotes eco-friendly tourism and responsible outdoor activities to preserve its pristine environment.

Chapter 1

Getting to Tromsø

By Air

Getting to Tromsø there by air is much easier than you might think. The anticipation of flying to such a unique destination adds an extra sense of excitement to the journey, as you soar toward the Arctic Circle. The moment you board your flight bound for Tromsø, it's as though the everyday world begins to slip away. Whether you're leaving from bustling Oslo or another European city, there's a growing sense of adventure in the air. Tromsø Airport (TOS) is well-connected, offering direct flights from cities such as Oslo, London, and Frankfurt, making it accessible despite its remote location. As you fly over the scenic landscapes of Norway, with its sprawling fjords, snow-capped mountains, and winding rivers, you start to get a glimpse of the natural beauty awaiting you.

When the plane begins its descent into Tromsø, emotions tend to bubble up. From your window, you'll see the icy blue waters of the fjords and the jagged mountains that frame the city. It's almost surreal—this isn't just any landing; it feels like you're arriving at the edge of the world. For many, the first sight of Tromsø from the air evokes a sense of awe and wonder. The isolation of the landscape combined with the rugged beauty of the Arctic North leaves an impression that's hard to shake. Stepping off the plane, you're greeted by the crisp, clean Arctic air, which feels invigorating, almost like a promise of the adventure ahead. Tromsø Airport is small and welcoming, which makes arriving here feel personal and intimate, much like the city itself. There's no sense of hustle and bustle; instead, there's a calmness that mirrors the natural surroundings.

One of the best parts about flying to Tromsø is how close the airport is to the city center. A short 10-minute drive will have you in the heart of Tromsø, where wooden houses meet the surrounding wilderness. That quick journey is filled with excitement, as you see the Arctic Cathedral in the distance or catch a glimpse of the cable car leading up to Mount Storsteinen. It's a reminder that even though Tromsø is a small city, it's full of captivating sights and experiences. flying to Tromsø is more than just a mode of transportation.The anticipation, the beauty from above, and the sheer thrill of landing in such a remote and extraordinary place stay with you, long after your plane touches down.

By Sea

Traveling to Tromsø by sea is something undeniably magical. It's a journey that feels like an adventure from the very start, offering a deeper connection to the stunning landscapes of northern Norway. Sailing into Tromsø isn't just about reaching a destination , it's about the experience, the slow approach, the moments of awe as the Arctic wilderness reveals itself. As you depart from ports further south, the world around you begins to transform. The coastline of Norway, with its rugged cliffs and deep blue fjords, gradually unfolds like a living, breathing postcard. Whether you're on a ferry, a cruise ship, or one of Norway's famed Hurtigruten coastal ships, you'll feel a growing sense of anticipation. The journey becomes part of the destination, as the endless horizon stretches before you, blending the deep hues of the sea with the pale sky. One of the most striking things about traveling by sea is the stillness. The water often looks like glass, reflecting the sky and surrounding mountains, creating a mirror-like effect that blurs the lines between reality and reflection. There's a quiet beauty in this solitude, a sense of peace as your ship glides through the Arctic waters. The further north you go, the more intense the natural beauty becomes. Fjords cut deep into the coastline, and mountains seem to rise straight out of the sea. You may even spot whales or dolphins along the way, their presence a reminder of the wild, untamed nature of the Arctic. The approach to Tromsø is slow, almost reverent. As the city comes into view, it feels like a reward after the long, meditative journey. The iconic Arctic Cathedral stands out against the backdrop of mountains, its triangular shape mirroring the sharp peaks that surround it. The bridges that connect Tromsø to the mainland and surrounding islands stretch across the water, a modern marvel in this ancient, untamed landscape.

There's a deep sense of history here, a feeling of following in the footsteps of explorers, fishermen, and traders who made their way north in search of new opportunities and adventure. Stepping off the ship, there's a moment of exhilaration. You're no longer just observing the beauty of Norway's Arctic, you're a part of it. The cool air hits your face, and you can feel the energy of Tromsø around you. The port is small but bustling, with the sounds of the sea mixing with the hum of city life. As you disembark, the charm of Tromsø's wooden buildings, the sight of the mountains surrounding you, and the thrill of knowing you've arrived in such a unique and remote place fills you with excitement.

By Land

The journey often begins in Norway's heartland, where the landscapes are already impressive but still familiar. Rolling hills and calm lakes pass by your window, but as you head north, the scenery starts to shift. The trees grow sparser, and the mountains begin to rise higher, their jagged peaks cutting into the sky. The world feels wilder with each passing hour.

For many, the trip by land means a long road trip. If you're driving, the adventure begins the moment you leave the last major city behind. The highways become narrower, and the traffic thins out, replaced by wide open roads that stretch endlessly toward the horizon. There's a sense of anticipation that grows with each bend in the road—what's around the next corner? Another mountain? A glacier-fed river? Every turn seems to reveal something new and unexpected. The drive itself is an experience of contrasts. One moment, you'll find yourself cruising alongside deep blue fjords, with towering cliffs on one side and water that looks almost otherworldly on the other. Next, you'll be weaving through mountain passes, where the air is crisp and clear, and the landscape feels untouched by time. You may pass through tiny villages, where red and yellow houses dot the landscape, offering a glimpse of life in this remote part of the world. If you're taking a train, the journey has a different kind of rhythm, but it's no less captivating. The Norwegian rail network can take you as far north as Narvik, just shy of Tromsø, where the final stretch is covered by bus. The trains wind their way through valleys, past snow-covered mountains, and along fjords so stunning that you can't help but stare out the window for hours on end.

And then, finally, as you approach Tromsø, the Arctic really starts to make itself known. The trees thin out completely, replaced by endless stretches of tundra. You may even see reindeer grazing by the side of the road, a reminder that you're entering a world that is truly unlike any other. The last stretch of the journey, whether by car or bus, brings a mix of excitement and quiet reflection. Tromsø isn't the kind of place you stumble upon; it's a destination that you reach with intention. There's a sense of accomplishment in the fact that you've made it this far, through some of the most remote and dramatic landscapes in Europe. And then, just when it feels like you've reached the end of the earth, the city of Tromsø appears small, but vibrant, nestled between the sea and the mountains. Arriving in Tromsø by land isn't just about the destination, it's about the journey. It's about the countless moments along the way that make you stop and catch your breath. It's the quiet roads, the wild landscapes, and the feeling of venturing deeper into the Arctic than you ever thought possible. By the time you step out into the crisp Arctic air and see the city spread out before you, you know you've arrived somewhere truly extraordinary. It's a journey that stays with you, long after you've left Tromsø behind.

Chapter 2

Accomodation

Luxury hotels

Radisson blu hotel Tromsø

Address: Tromsø, Norway 9259 Sjøgata 7

Telephone: +47 77 60 00 00

Overview

The Radisson Blu Hotel Tromsø stands as a welcoming beacon amid the breathtaking landscapes of Tromsø. Located on Sjøgata, this hotel offers more than just a place to stay, it provides an immersive experience in one of Norway's most enchanting locations. Imagine waking up to the sight of the sparkling Tromsø Sound and the majestic Arctic fjords. With its contemporary design and warm, inviting atmosphere, the Radisson Blu is an ideal haven for travelers seeking both luxury and comfort. Here, every detail is thoughtfully curated to ensure that your stay is nothing short of exceptional.

Room Features

Each room at the Radisson Blu Hotel Tromsø is a sanctuary of modern elegance. The rooms are adorned with stylish furnishings and soothing color palettes, designed to create a serene escape after a

29

day of exploration. Guests can choose from a range of room types, including standard rooms, suites, and business-friendly options.

Standard Rooms: These rooms offer comfortable beds with plush linens, flat-screen TVs, and cozy workspaces. Large windows invite natural light and provide stunning views of the city or the surrounding fjords.

Suites: For those seeking a touch of extra luxury, the suites feature separate living areas, premium bedding, and upgraded amenities. Some suites even boast panoramic views that capture the essence of Tromsø's natural beauty.

Business Rooms: Equipped with ergonomic workspaces and high-speed internet, these rooms cater to professionals who need to stay productive while on the road.

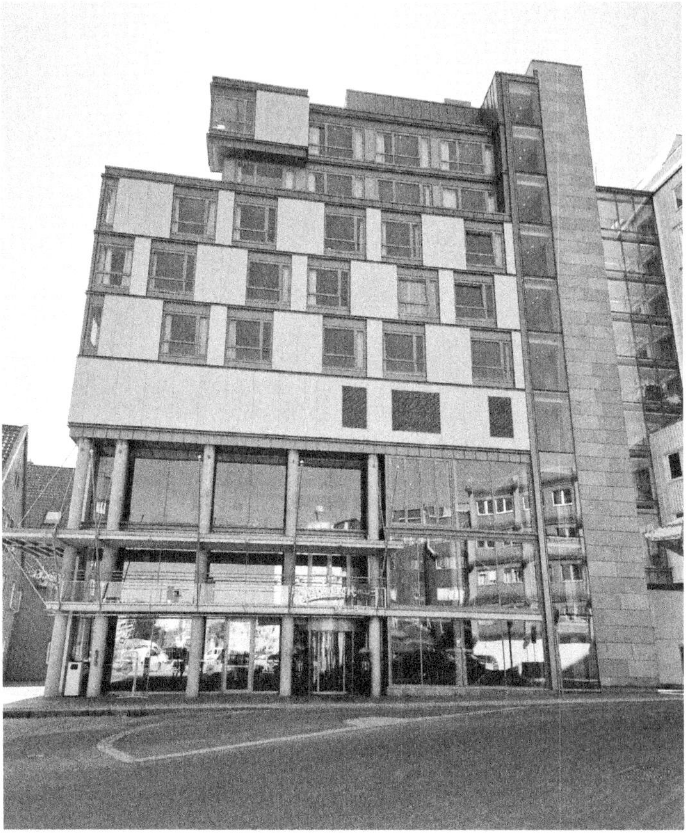

Property Amenities

The Radisson Blu Hotel Tromsø is equipped with a range of amenities designed to enhance your stay:

Dining: Enjoy a delicious meal at the hotel's restaurant, which offers a diverse menu featuring local and international cuisine. Whether you're starting your day with a hearty breakfast or winding down with a delightful dinner, the dining experience here is sure to impress.

Bar: The hotel's bar is the perfect spot to relax with a cocktail or a glass of wine. Its cozy atmosphere is ideal for unwinding after a day of sightseeing or for catching up with friends and family.

Fitness Center: Maintain your workout routine with the well-equipped fitness center, offering a variety of exercise equipment and a motivating environment.

Meeting Facilities: For business travelers, the hotel provides versatile meeting and conference spaces, complete with modern audio-visual equipment and high-speed internet.

Free Wi-Fi: Stay connected throughout the hotel with complimentary high-speed internet access.

Pet-Friendly: The Radisson Blu Hotel Tromsø is pet-friendly, allowing you to bring along your furry friends on your journey.

Pricing

The rates at Radisson Blu Hotel Tromsø vary depending on the season and room type. On average:

Standard Rooms: Prices typically start around NOK 1,200 to NOK 1,800 per night.

Suites: Expect to pay between NOK 2,500 and NOK 4,000 per night, depending on the suite type and view.

Business Rooms: Rates for business rooms generally range from NOK 1,500 to NOK 2,200 per night.

The hotel often offers special packages and discounts, so it's a good idea to check their website or contact the front desk for the best rates during your planned stay.

Clarion hotel the edge

Address: Tromsø ,Norway 9008, Kaigata 6.
Telephone: +47 77 66 84 00

Overview

Clarion Hotel The Edge, offers a vibrant blend of modern design and warm hospitality. From its prime location on Kaigata, this hotel stands as a gateway to Tromsø's stunning natural beauty and lively city life. With a name that suggests a touch of adventure, The Edge lives up to its promise, offering an exhilarating stay that captures the essence of Arctic charm. Imagine starting your day with breathtaking views of the surrounding fjords and snow-capped peaks, and ending it with a taste of local delicacies in a contemporary yet cozy setting.

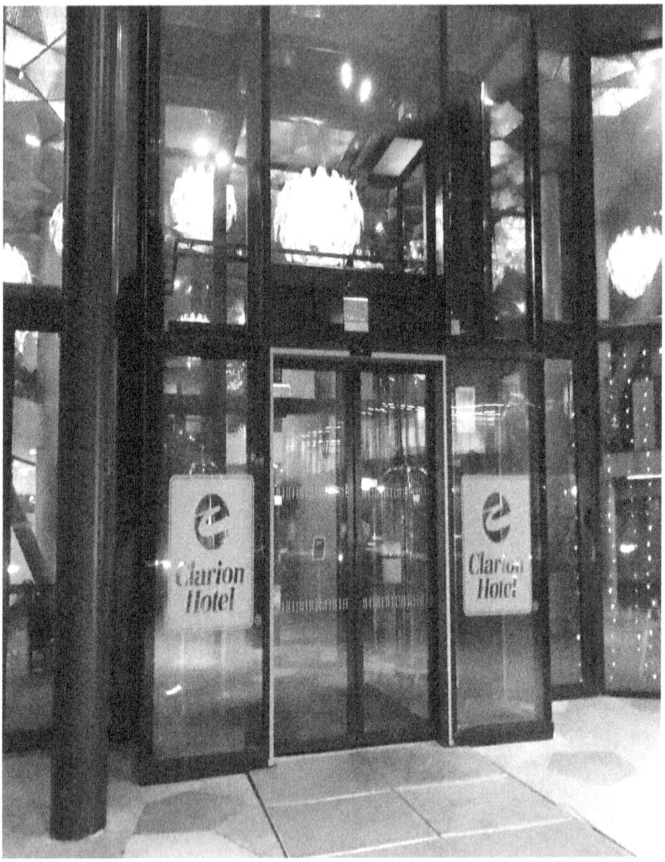
Clarion
Hotel
Hotel

Room Features

The rooms at Clarion Hotel The Edge are crafted to provide both comfort and style. Each space is designed with sleek, modern aesthetics and thoughtful amenities, ensuring that every guest feels right at home.

Standard Rooms: These rooms offer a comfortable retreat with plush bedding, stylish décor, and large windows that let in natural light. Enjoy amenities like a flat-screen TV, complimentary Wi-Fi, and a work desk, making it easy to relax or stay productive.

Superior Rooms: Upgraded to offer a bit more space and luxury, Superior Rooms feature enhanced furnishings, better views, and additional comforts like a Nespresso coffee machine and premium toiletries.

Suites: For a truly indulgent experience, the suites at The Edge provide a separate living area, elegant design elements, and stunning panoramic views of the Arctic landscape. Perfect for special occasions or extended stays, these suites come with extra perks like bathrobes and slippers.

Property Amenities

Clarion Hotel The Edge is equipped with a range of amenities designed to make your stay as enjoyable and convenient as possible:

Dining: Start your day with a sumptuous breakfast buffet featuring a variety of local and international options. For lunch and dinner, the hotel's restaurant serves a selection of delectable dishes that showcase regional flavors and fresh ingredients.

Bar: The stylish bar is a perfect place to unwind after a day of exploring. Sip on expertly crafted cocktails, local beers, or a glass of fine wine while enjoying the relaxed ambiance and great company.

Fitness Center: Keep up with your fitness routine in the well-equipped gym, offering modern exercise equipment and a motivating environment to help you stay active.

Meeting Facilities: For business travelers, the hotel provides versatile meeting rooms and event spaces, complete with the latest technology and comfortable settings to host successful meetings or gatherings.

Free Wi-Fi: Stay connected throughout the hotel with complimentary high-speed internet access, ensuring that you can easily keep in touch with family, friends, or colleagues.

Rooftop Bar: One of the hotel's standout features is its rooftop bar, where you can enjoy a drink while taking in panoramic views of Tromsø and the surrounding fjords—an ideal spot to watch the Northern Lights if you're visiting during the right season.

Pricing

Rates at Clarion Hotel The Edge can vary based on the time of year, room type, and booking details. On average:

Standard Rooms: Prices typically start around NOK 1,200 to NOK 1,800 per night.

Superior Rooms: Expect to pay between NOK 1,800 and NOK 2,500 per night.

Suites: Suite rates generally range from NOK 2,800 to NOK 4,500 per night.

The hotel often offers special packages and promotions, so it's worth checking their website or contacting them directly for the best available rates during your stay.

Scandic ishavshotel

Address: Tromso Fredrik langes gate 2, 9008 Norway

Telephone: +47 77 66 64 01

Overview

Scandic Ishavshotel offers an extraordinary blend of contemporary comfort and stunning natural beauty, nestled in the heart of Tromsø. Situated right by the harbor, this hotel provides unparalleled views of the fjords and mountains, creating a picturesque backdrop for your stay. Whether you're here for a short visit or an extended getaway, Scandic Ishavshotel welcomes you with a warm, inviting atmosphere that reflects the charm of Arctic Norway. Imagine sipping your morning coffee while gazing out at the serene waters or unwinding in style after a day of exploration.

Room Features

The rooms at Scandic Ishavshotel are designed with a focus on comfort and style, ensuring a restful stay amidst Tromsø's captivating scenery.

Standard Rooms: These rooms are well-appointed with comfortable beds, tasteful décor, and large windows that offer beautiful views of either the city or the harbor. Each room includes a flat-screen TV, free Wi-Fi, and a workspace, making it ideal for both relaxation and productivity.

Superior Rooms: Enjoy enhanced comfort and space in the Superior Rooms, which feature upgraded furnishings, better views, and additional amenities such as a coffee maker and premium toiletries. These rooms provide a more luxurious retreat, perfect for those looking to indulge a bit more.

Suites: The suites at Scandic Ishavshotel provide a luxurious escape with separate living areas, expansive windows, and stunning panoramic views. Ideal for special occasions or longer stays, suites come with added touches like bathrobes, slippers, and a mini-bar.

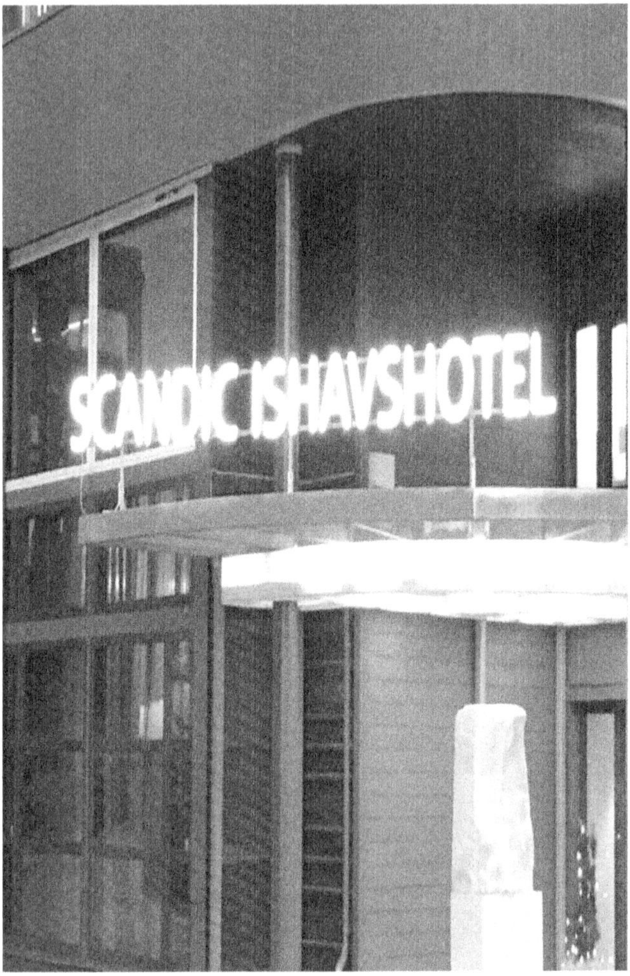
SCANDIC ISHAVSHOTEL

Property Amenities

Scandic Ishavshotel is equipped with a variety of amenities designed to make your stay as enjoyable and convenient as possible:

Dining: The hotel's restaurant offers a delightful array of dishes made from fresh, local ingredients. Start your day with a hearty breakfast buffet, and enjoy lunch or dinner with a view of the harbor. The menu features both Norwegian specialties and international favorites.

Bar: Relax in the hotel bar with a selection of drinks, from craft beers to fine wines. The bar provides a cozy setting to unwind after a day of sightseeing or to socialize with fellow travelers.

Fitness Center: Keep up with your fitness routine in the well-equipped gym, which offers a range of exercise equipment to help you stay active during your stay.

Meeting Facilities: For business guests, the hotel provides modern meeting rooms and conference facilities. Equipped with the latest technology, these spaces are ideal for hosting meetings, presentations, and events.

Free Wi-Fi: Enjoy complimentary high-speed internet access throughout the hotel, making it easy to stay connected with family, friends, and work.

Pet-Friendly: Scandic Ishavshotel welcomes pets, allowing you to bring your furry friends along on your Arctic adventure.

Pricing

Rates at Scandic Ishavshotel can vary depending on the time of year, room type, and booking details. On average:

Standard Rooms: Prices generally start around NOK 1,200 to NOK 1,800 per night.

Superior Rooms: Expect to pay between NOK 1,800 and NOK 2,500 per night.

Suites: Suite rates typically range from NOK 2,800 to NOK 4,000 per night.

Quality hotel strand Gjøvik

Address: Gjøvik 2815, Elvegata 3-4, Norway
Telephone: +47 61 13 20 00

Overview

Step into a world of comfort and charm at the Quality Hotel Strand Gjøvik, where warm Norwegian hospitality meets modern convenience. Situated in the heart of Gjøvik, this hotel is a beacon of relaxation and style, offering a cozy retreat whether you're visiting for business, leisure, or a special occasion. The moment you walk through the doors, you'll be greeted by a welcoming atmosphere that reflects the essence of Gjøvik's vibrant community and stunning surroundings. Imagine unwinding in a beautifully appointed room after a day of exploring or attending an event, knowing that every detail of your stay has been thoughtfully crafted to ensure your utmost comfort.

Room Features

At Quality Hotel Strand Gjøvik, each room is designed to be a peaceful sanctuary, blending contemporary elegance with homey touches.

Standard Rooms: These inviting spaces are perfect for a restful stay. With comfortable beds, tasteful décor, and large windows allowing natural light to fill the room, you'll find everything you need for a relaxing retreat. Each room is equipped with a flat-screen TV, free Wi-Fi, and a cozy work desk, ideal for both leisure and productivity.

Superior Rooms: For a touch more luxury, Superior Rooms offer enhanced amenities and more space. Enjoy additional comforts such as a coffee maker, premium toiletries, and a seating area where you can relax and take in the views of the surrounding area. These rooms are designed to make your stay even more enjoyable and restful.

Suites: The suites at Quality Hotel Strand Gjøvik provide a higher level of indulgence with separate living areas and extra space. Perfect for longer stays or special occasions, the suites include features like plush bathrobes, a mini-bar, and breathtaking views. The thoughtful design ensures that you experience the pinnacle of comfort and style.

Property Amenities

Quality Hotel Strand Gjøvik offers a range of amenities that cater to both relaxation and convenience, ensuring that your stay is as enjoyable as possible.

Dining: Start your day with a delicious breakfast buffet featuring a variety of fresh, local options to fuel your adventures. For lunch and dinner, the hotel's restaurant offers a selection of tasty dishes prepared with care, showcasing the best of Norwegian cuisine in a comfortable setting.

Bar: Unwind with a drink at the hotel's bar, where you can enjoy a selection of beverages, from refreshing cocktails to local beers. The bar is a cozy spot to relax after a busy day, socialize with friends, or simply enjoy a quiet evening.

Fitness Center: Stay active in the hotel's well-equipped gym, which offers modern exercise equipment and a motivating environment to help you keep up with your fitness routine.

Meeting Facilities: For business travelers, the hotel provides versatile meeting rooms and conference facilities equipped with the latest technology. These spaces are designed to host successful meetings, seminars, and events, ensuring a productive and pleasant experience.

Free Wi-Fi: Stay connected with complimentary high-speed internet access throughout the hotel, allowing you to keep in touch with family, friends, or colleagues.

Spa and Wellness: Enjoy a bit of pampering with access to the hotel's spa facilities, where you can indulge in treatments designed to relax and rejuvenate you.

Pricing

The rates at Quality Hotel Strand Gjøvik vary depending on the time of year, room type, and availability. Here's a general idea of what you can expect:

Standard Rooms: Typically range from NOK 1,000 to NOK 1,500 per night. These rates offer excellent value for a comfortable and well-equipped room.

Superior Rooms: Usually priced between NOK 1,500 and NOK 2,200 per night. These rooms provide extra space and upgraded amenities for those seeking a bit more luxury.

Suites: Expect to pay from NOK 2,500 to NOK 3,500 per night. The suites offer an enhanced level of comfort and sophistication, ideal for special occasions or extended stays.

Thon hotel Tromsø

Address: Norway, Tromso 9008,Groennegata

Telephone: +47 77 69 80 50

Overview

Welcome to Thon Hotel Tromsø, where comfort and convenience come together in the heart of Tromsø. Located on Grønnegata, this hotel offers a blend of modern amenities and warm hospitality, making it an ideal choice for both business and leisure travelers. Whether you're here to explore the breathtaking landscapes or attend a conference, Thon Hotel Tromsø provides a welcoming environment designed to make your stay enjoyable and stress-free.

From the moment you step inside, you'll appreciate the hotel's attention to detail. The cozy and contemporary rooms are perfect for unwinding after a day of exploring or meetings. With a dedicated team at the 24-hour front desk ready to assist you and a range of thoughtful amenities, your comfort is always a priority.

Property amenities:
- Paid public parking nearby
- Free High Speed Internet (WiFi)
- Free breakfast
- Taxi service
- Conference facilities

- Meeting rooms
- Baggage storage
- Non-smoking hotel
- Parking
- Wifi
- Breakfast buffet
- Wine / champagne
- 24-hour front desk
- Laundry service

Room features

- Air conditioning
- Minibar
- Flatscreen TV

Pricing

Thon Hotel Tromsø offers competitive rates that vary based on the season and room type. Here's a general guide to their pricing:

Standard Rooms: Generally priced between NOK 1,200 and NOK 1,800 per night. These rooms provide all the essential comforts and are equipped with modern amenities to ensure a pleasant stay.

Deluxe Rooms: Typically range from NOK 1,800 to NOK 2,500 per night. Offering extra space and enhanced features, these rooms are perfect for guests looking for a bit more luxury and comfort.

Suites: Expect rates from NOK 2,500 to NOK 3,500 per night. Suites at Thon Hotel Tromsø provide additional space and premium amenities, ideal for those seeking a more indulgent experience.

Tromsø Lodge and camping

Address: Tromsdalen 9020, Arthur Arntzens veg 10, Norway

Telephone: +47 77 63 80 37

Overview

Tromsø Lodge & Camping offers a unique blend of natural beauty and cozy accommodation, providing a refreshing escape from the hustle and bustle of city life. Nestled in the serene Tromsdalen area, this lodge and camping site is perfect for travelers seeking a tranquil retreat surrounded by Norway's stunning landscapes. Whether you're an outdoor enthusiast or someone simply looking to unwind, Tromsø Lodge & Camping provides a variety of lodging options that cater to different preferences. From charming lodges to well-equipped cabins and picturesque camping spots, each option is designed to enhance your experience of Tromsø's natural splendor. The lodge itself is designed to offer comfort while maintaining a close connection with the great outdoors. Enjoy the rustic charm of the area while benefiting from modern conveniences and facilities. The location provides easy access to Tromsø's attractions, making it an ideal base for exploring the region's natural wonders and cultural highlights.

Pricing

Tromsø Lodge & Camping offers a range of pricing options to suit different needs and budgets:

Cabins: Prices for cabins typically range from NOK 1,200 to NOK 2,000 per night. These cabins provide a cozy and comfortable stay with amenities like private bathrooms, kitchen facilities, and scenic views.

Lodges: Expect to pay between NOK 2,000 and NOK 3,000 per night for lodges. These accommodations offer more space and added comfort, perfect for families or groups looking for a more luxurious stay.

Camping Sites: For those who prefer a more outdoorsy experience, camping sites are available at rates starting from NOK 300 to NOK 600 per night. These sites are well-equipped and provide a great way to enjoy Tromsø's natural surroundings

Property amenities:

- Free parking

- Free High Speed Internet (WiFi)
- Sauna
- Bar / lounge
- Bicycle rental
- Hiking
- Pets Allowed (Dog / Pet Friendly)
- Taxi service
- Electric vehicle charging station
- Wifi
- Coffee shop
- Breakfast available
- Outdoor dining area
- Snack bar
- Wine / champagne
- Skiing
- Walking tours
- Baggage storage
- Non-smoking hotel
- Outdoor furniture

Room features:

- Allergy-free room
- Soundproof rooms
- Dining area
- Housekeeping
- Seating area
- Coffee / tea maker
- Cable / satellite TV

Enter Amalie hotel

Address: 9008 Tromsø,Sjøgata 5b Norway
Telephone: +47 77 66 48 00

Overview

Amalie Hotel offers a blend of warmth and convenience right in the heart of Tromsø. Located on Sjøgata, this charming hotel provides a comfortable and friendly atmosphere ideal for travelers looking to explore the Arctic city. With its welcoming environment and central location, it's a perfect base for discovering Tromsø's attractions and vibrant culture.

Property Amenities

Free High-Speed Internet (WiFi): Stay connected throughout your visit with complimentary high-speed internet access.

Free Breakfast: Start your day right with a delicious breakfast served each morning, featuring a variety of options to suit different tastes.

24-Hour Front Desk: The attentive staff are available around the clock to assist with any needs or requests you may have.

Baggage Storage: Convenient storage for your luggage before check-in or after check-out.

Non-Smoking Hotel: Enjoy a smoke-free environment throughout the property.

Elevator: Easy access to all floors of the hotel for added convenience.

Laundry Service: On-site laundry facilities to keep your clothes fresh and clean.

Taxi Service: Arrangements can be made for local taxi services to make your travels around Tromsø hassle-free.

Room Features

Air Conditioning: Stay comfortable no matter the weather with air conditioning in all rooms.

Flat-Screen TV: Enjoy your favorite shows and movies on a modern flat-screen television.

Minibar: Keep refreshments and snacks within reach with a well-stocked minibar.

Desk and Chair: A dedicated workspace for those who need to catch up on emails or plan their next adventure.

Safe: Secure your valuables and important belongings during your stay.

Coffee/Tea Maker: Brew your own coffee or tea for a relaxing start to your day.

Private Bathroom: Each room includes a private bathroom with a shower or bathtub, ensuring comfort and privacy.

Pricing

Standard Rooms: Typically range from NOK 1,100 to NOK 1,500 per night, offering essential amenities and a comfortable stay.

Superior Rooms: Priced between NOK 1,500 and NOK 2,000 per night, these rooms provide additional space and enhanced features.

Family Rooms: Generally from NOK 2,000 to NOK 2,500 per night, designed to accommodate families or groups with extra space and comfort.

St Elisabeth suites & Spa

Address: 9007 Tromsø, Mellomvegen 50, Norway
Telephone: +47 92 04 54 60

Overview

This exquisite retreat offers a serene escape with its blend of sophisticated accommodations and rejuvenating spa services. Whether you're in Tromsø for a relaxing getaway or an adventurous exploration of the Arctic, this hotel provides a perfect balance of comfort and indulgence. From the moment you arrive, you're enveloped in an atmosphere of calm and elegance. The suites are designed with a keen eye for detail, ensuring that each guest experiences a sense of tranquility and refined luxury. The on-site spa offers a range of treatments to help you unwind and recharge after a day of discovering Tromsø's natural wonders.

Property Amenities

Full-Service Spa: Pamper yourself with a variety of treatments and therapies designed to rejuvenate and relax. The spa offers massages, facials, and wellness packages to enhance your stay.

Free High-Speed Internet (WiFi): Stay connected with complimentary high-speed internet available throughout the property.

Free Breakfast: Enjoy a delightful breakfast each morning, featuring a selection of fresh and locally-sourced ingredients.

Fitness Center: Keep up with your fitness routine in the well-equipped gym, complete with modern exercise equipment.

24-Hour Front Desk: The friendly staff are available around the clock to assist with any requests or provide local information.

Concierge Service: Personalized assistance with booking tours, arranging transportation, or making restaurant reservations.

On-Site Parking: Convenient parking facilities are available for guests traveling by car.

Non-Smoking Property: A smoke-free environment throughout the hotel ensures a clean and fresh atmosphere.

Room Features

Luxurious Suites: Each suite is thoughtfully designed to provide a blend of comfort and elegance, featuring stylish décor and high-end furnishings.

Private Balcony: Enjoy panoramic views of Tromsø and its stunning landscapes from your private balcony.

Flat-Screen TV: Relax and unwind with a range of entertainment options on a modern flat-screen television.

Minibar: A well-stocked minibar is available for your convenience, offering a selection of beverages and snacks.

Air Conditioning: Stay comfortable year-round with individual climate control in each suite.

Coffee/Tea Maker: Brew a fresh cup of coffee or tea at your leisure with in-room coffee and tea-making facilities.

Spacious Living Area: Each suite includes a comfortable living area, perfect for relaxing after a day of sightseeing.

Luxurious Bedding: Enjoy a restful night's sleep on high-quality bedding and plush pillows.

Private Bathroom: Each suite features a stylish private bathroom with a shower or bathtub, complete with premium toiletries and bathrobes.

Pricing

Suites: Rates generally range from NOK 2,500 to NOK 3,500 per night. Pricing may vary based on the season, room type, and availability. For the most accurate rates and to make a reservation, it's recommended to contact St. Elisabeth Suites & Spa directly or visit their website.

Budget friendly hotels

Smarthotel Tromsø

Address: 9008 tromø, Vestregata 6, Norway
Telephone: +47 41 53 65 00

Overview

Smarthotel Tromsø is a modern, budget-friendly accommodation located in the heart of Tromsø, making it the perfect base for travelers looking to explore the Arctic city. Known for its simplicity, efficiency, and value for money, this hotel offers the essentials needed for a comfortable stay without unnecessary frills. Its prime location allows easy access to many of Tromsø's must-see attractions, including the Polar Museum, Arctic Cathedral, and the city's lively restaurants and bars.

Smarthotel Tromsø has become a go-to option for both leisure and business travelers due to its affordability and convenience. Whether you're here to witness the magical Northern Lights, embark on an adventure-filled Arctic experience, or simply relax in Tromsø's natural beauty, the hotel serves as a cozy, practical haven.

Property Amenities

Free High-Speed Internet (WiFi): Stay connected with reliable, fast internet throughout the hotel.

24-Hour Front Desk: The friendly staff is available around the clock to assist you with any inquiries, ensuring your stay is as smooth as possible.

Express Check-In/Check-Out: For travelers on the go, the hotel offers quick and efficient check-in and check-out services, saving you time.

Snack Bar: A convenient snack bar is located within the hotel, offering light meals, drinks, and snacks for guests on the move.

Self-Service Breakfast: Start your day with a simple, but fresh buffet breakfast that includes a range of items like bread, cereals, fruits, and juices.

Laundry Services: For longer stays, guests can take advantage of laundry facilities to keep their clothes fresh.

Non-Smoking Property: The entire hotel is non-smoking, ensuring a clean and pleasant environment for all guests.

Room Features

Compact Design: Smarthotel Tromsø offers small but well-designed rooms that make efficient use of space. Each room is cozy and functional, perfect for travelers looking for a minimalist yet comfortable stay.

Comfortable Bed: Enjoy a restful sleep in a high-quality bed with soft linens and pillows, ensuring you wake up refreshed and ready to explore Tromsø.

Flat-Screen TV: Stay entertained with a flat-screen TV in each room, featuring a range of local and international channels.

Work Desk: For those traveling for business, each room includes a work desk, providing a quiet space to focus on tasks.

Private Bathroom: The rooms come with private, compact bathrooms equipped with modern fixtures, including a shower, toilet, and complimentary toiletries.

Air Conditioning: Climate control in each room allows you to adjust the temperature to your liking, keeping you comfortable throughout your stay.

Blackout Curtains: Ideal for getting rest during Tromsø's bright summers or dark winters, blackout curtains ensure a peaceful and quiet night's sleep.

Pricing

Smarthotel Tromsø is known for offering great value, with room rates typically ranging between NOK 600 to NOK 1,000 per night depending on the time of year and room availability. Prices can fluctuate during peak seasons, such as during the Northern Lights season and summer months, so it's recommended to book in advance.

Enter city hotel

Address: Tromsø 9008, Grønnegata 48, Norway
Telephone: +47 77 78 10 50

Overview
Enter City Hotel is a modern, comfortable, and conveniently located accommodation in the center of Tromsø. Perfectly suited for both short stays and extended visits, this hotel offers apartment-style rooms with fully equipped kitchenettes, allowing

guests the flexibility to cook their own meals. This feature makes it an ideal choice for families, business travelers, and those looking for a home-like atmosphere during their stay.

The hotel's location is one of its best assets, placing guests within walking distance of Tromsø's key attractions, including the Polar Museum, Tromsø Cathedral, and the vibrant waterfront. The hotel combines the convenience of self-catering with the comforts of hotel service, ensuring guests have everything they need for a relaxing and enjoyable stay.

Pricing

Room rates at Enter City Hotel vary depending on the season, length of stay, and room type. On average, prices typically range from NOK 1,000 to NOK 1,800 per night, with lower rates during off-peak periods and higher prices during the busy Northern Lights and summer tourist seasons. Extended stays and early bookings often come with discounts, making it a great choice for those planning longer trips to Tromsø.

Property amenities:
- Paid private parking on-site
- Free High Speed Internet (WiFi)
- Complimentary Instant Coffee
- Highchairs available
- 24-hour security
- Baggage storage
- 24-hour check-in
- Clothes dryer
- Parking garage
- Wifi
- Complimentary tea
- Non-smoking hotel
- First aid kit
- Laundry service
- Self-serve laundry
- Washing machine

Room features:

- Allergy-free room
- Blackout curtains
- Dining area
- Housekeeping
- Seating area
- Coffee / tea maker
- Flatscreen TV
- Hair dryer
- Wardrobe / closet
- Tile / marble floor
- Kitchenette
- Oven
- Refrigerator
- Stovetop
- Electric kettle
- Kitchenware

Comfort hotel Xpress Tromsø

Address: Tromsø 9008, Grønnegata 35, Norway
Telephone: +47 77 60 05 50

Overview

Comfort Hotel Xpress Tromsø is designed for the traveler who values efficiency, affordability, and fun. It offers the essentials: clean, modern rooms with all the necessities like comfortable beds, flat-screen TVs, and free Wi-Fi. The rooms may be simple, but they are sleek and cozy, offering a perfect spot to relax after a day spent exploring Tromsø's wonders.

There's no in-house restaurant, but Tromsø's buzzing food scene is just steps away, so you're encouraged to experience the local culture. Plus, with no daily room cleaning (unless requested), the hotel offers an eco-conscious stay without sacrificing comfort, aligning with modern travelers who care about their carbon footprint.

Human Connection
Staying at Comfort Hotel Xpress feels more like staying at a friend's place than a typical hotel. You're invited to enjoy the communal areas, designed with modern furniture and cool lighting that fosters a relaxed atmosphere. Whether you're here to meet new people, swap stories of your adventures, or unwind with a good book, these spaces feel welcoming and warm. It's these small touches of community that make the hotel memorable.

Property Amenities

- Free High-Speed Wi-Fi
- 24-hour front desk
- Self-service check-in/out kiosks
- Communal lounge and workspace
- Luggage storage
- Eco-friendly policies (no daily cleaning unless requested)
- Breakfast options available at nearby restaurants

Room Features

- Comfortable double or twin beds
- Modern, minimalist decor
- Flat-screen TV
- Free Wi-Fi
- Desk and chair
- En-suite bathroom with shower
- Blackout curtains (a lifesaver during those midnight sun nights)

Pricing

Comfort Hotel Xpress Tromsø is all about offering great value for money. Prices are affordable, especially for its central location, with rates starting from NOK 700 to NOK 1,200 per night, depending on the season and room type. It's perfect for travelers who want to experience the magic of Tromsø without breaking the bank, offering a place that feels more like a home than just another stop on the map.

Skansen hotell Tromsø

Address: Tromsø 9008, Storgata 105 Norway

Telephone: +47 77 62 95 00

Overview

Skansen Hotell blends simplicity with comfort, offering guests a delightful, stress-free experience. The hotel's convenient location on Storgata puts you right in the center of the action, with Tromsø's main attractions just a short walk away. You'll be close to the Polar Museum, the Arctic Cathedral, and the bustling harbor, giving you easy access to everything Tromsø has to offer.

With its traditional Norwegian hospitality, Skansen Hotell provides guests with a laid-back yet intimate atmosphere. Whether you're relaxing in your room or chatting with the staff in the cozy common areas, you'll feel at home here. It's the kind of place that's perfect for solo travelers, couples, and families looking for both comfort and affordability in the Arctic capital.

Property Amenities

Free High-Speed Wi-Fi: Stay connected throughout your visit, whether you're working remotely or sharing your travel experiences with friends and family.

Complimentary Breakfast: Start your day off right with a delicious buffet breakfast served in the cozy dining area, featuring a selection of fresh breads, cheeses, fruits, and Norwegian specialties.

Free Parking: A rarity in Tromsø, the hotel offers free parking for guests, a convenient perk for those traveling by car.

Luggage Storage: Perfect for guests who want to explore the city after checking out, without the burden of carrying bags.

24-Hour Front Desk: Friendly, helpful staff are available around the clock to assist with any inquiries, recommendations, or travel tips.

Room Features

Each of the rooms at Skansen Hotell is designed to provide a warm, restful space for guests. They may not be extravagantly luxurious, but the rooms are clean, cozy, and well-appointed with everything you need for a comfortable stay.

Comfortable Beds: Soft, plush bedding ensures a great night's sleep after long days of Arctic adventures.

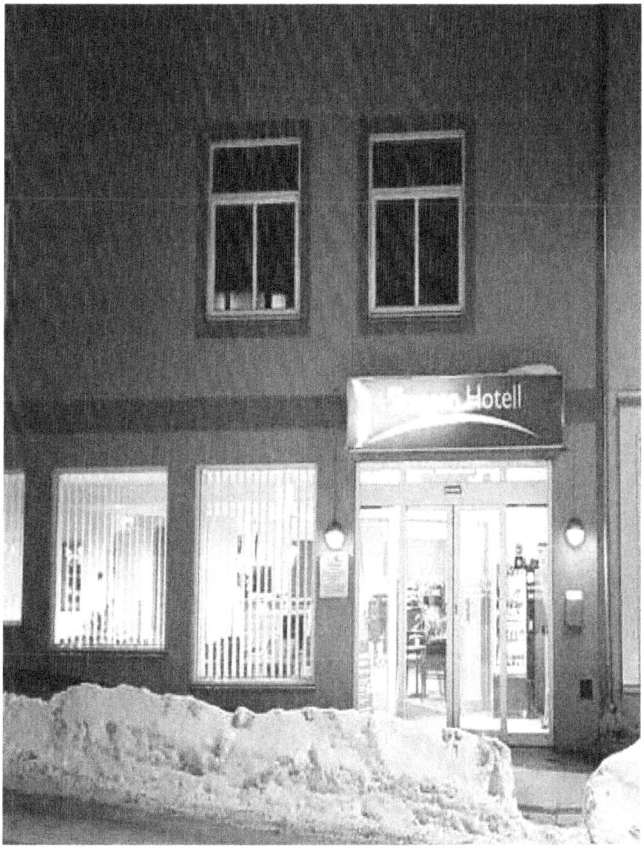
Hotell

Private Bathrooms: All rooms feature en-suite bathrooms with showers, ensuring privacy and convenience.

Flat-Screen TV: Unwind with some entertainment in the evenings, or catch up on local news and weather updates.

Desk and Chair: If you need to get some work done or plan your itinerary, the in-room workspace makes it easy.

Large Windows: Many rooms offer scenic views of Tromsø's city streets or nearby mountains, letting you feel connected to the vibrant surroundings.

Pricing

Skansen Hotell Tromsø offers excellent value for money, especially considering its central location and warm, welcoming ambiance. Prices typically range from NOK 800 to NOK 1,300 per night, depending on the room type and the season. This makes it an attractive option for budget-conscious travelers who don't want to compromise on comfort or convenience.

Enter backpack hotel

Address: Tromsø 9008, Parkgata 4, Norway

Telephone: +47 77 66 83 00

Overview

The enter Backpack Hotel is more than just a place to rest your head, it's a base for the curious traveler. With its strategic location just a short walk from Tromsø's main attractions, including the iconic

Arctic Cathedral, the Polar Museum, and the lively harbor, you'll never be far from the action. Step outside and explore the city's charming streets, or embark on one of Tromsø's many outdoor adventures, like chasing the Northern Lights, dog sledding, or whale watching.

What makes this hotel special is its relaxed, laid-back atmosphere. The staff are friendly and always ready to offer local tips, helping you make the most out of your time in Tromsø. The enter Backpack Hotel is where you'll find comfort without breaking the bank, with clean facilities and a welcoming environment that makes it feel like a home away from home.

Property Amenities

Free High-Speed Wi-Fi: Stay connected during your travels, whether you're planning your next adventure or sharing your Tromsø experiences on social media.

Communal Kitchen: Guests can use the well-equipped kitchen to prepare meals, saving money and offering a chance to share cooking experiences with other travelers.

Lounge and Common Areas: Relax after a day of exploration in the cozy lounge, where you can unwind, meet fellow travelers, or even exchange stories of your Arctic adventures.

Laundry Facilities: Ideal for those on extended trips, the hotel offers laundry services to keep your clothes fresh during your stay.

Luggage Storage: Drop off your bags and explore Tromsø, even if you arrive early or have a late departure.

Room Features

Enter Backpack Hotel offers a range of accommodation options to suit different needs and budgets. Whether you're looking for privacy or are happy to bunk in a shared room, the hotel provides a clean, comfortable stay.

Private Rooms: For those seeking more privacy, the hotel offers simple yet comfortable rooms with private bathrooms. These rooms are perfect for couples or solo travelers wanting a bit of space.

Dormitory-Style Rooms: Shared rooms are available for travelers looking for the most budget-friendly option. The dorms are well-maintained and provide lockers for secure storage of personal items.

Comfortable Beds: Each room or dorm comes with soft, comfortable bedding to ensure you get a good night's sleep after exploring Tromsø.

Clean Shared Facilities: Dorm guests can access shared bathrooms, which are cleaned regularly to ensure a pleasant experience for all visitors.

Pricing

Enter Backpack Hotel is known for offering great value in a city where accommodation prices can be steep. Private rooms typically range from NOK 800 to NOK 1,200 per night, depending on the season, while shared dormitory beds can be as affordable as NOK 300 to NOK 500 per night. The pricing makes it an excellent choice for backpackers, budget travelers, and anyone looking to save on accommodation while enjoying all the experiences Tromsø has to offer.

Booking tips and website

When booking accommodations in Tromsø, there are a few key tips and strategies to keep in mind to ensure you get the best experience possible, whether you're planning a luxurious stay or a more budget-friendly visit. Here's what you should know:

Booking Tips for Tromsø

1. Book Early for Peak Seasons: Tromsø is especially popular during the winter months when travelers flock to witness the Northern Lights and participate in winter activities. If you plan to visit during the Northern Lights season (November to February), make sure to book well in advance. Hotels, especially those with scenic views or proximity to attractions, fill up quickly. Booking 6 to 9 months ahead is ideal.

2. Look for Special Deals: Tromsø hotels often offer special deals during the off-peak months (spring and autumn). These packages might include discounts on long stays or bundled experiences, such as dog sledding or guided tours. Signing up for hotel newsletters or travel deal platforms can alert you to these offers.

3. Use Comparison Sites: Before committing to any booking, use travel comparison websites such as Booking.com, Expedia, or Hotels.com. They not only give you price comparisons but also offer guest reviews that provide valuable insights. Some platforms also offer rewards or cashback for frequent bookings.

4. Consider Local Booking Platforms: Some local Norwegian platforms or the hotel's own website might offer better deals than international booking platforms. For example, booking directly through Nordic Choice Hotels or Scandic's official websites often guarantees better cancellation policies or additional perks like free breakfast or parking.

5. Flexible Cancellation Policies: Tromsø's weather can be unpredictable, with changes in flight schedules or tour availability. Opt for accommodations that provide flexible or free cancellation policies so that you can adapt your travel plans if necessary.

6. Read Guest Reviews: Focus on guest reviews, especially recent ones. Pay attention to comments about cleanliness, service, and location. Many times, the photos provided by guests give a more accurate depiction than those found on hotel websites.

7. Consider Location: If you're in Tromsø for outdoor activities or festivals, choose accommodations close to the city center or main transport hubs to save on commuting time. On the other hand, if you prefer a more serene experience, there are cabins and lodges slightly outside the city that offer tranquility and picturesque landscapes.

8. Check for Hidden Costs: Some hotels in Tromsø may charge extra for amenities such as parking, Wi-Fi, or use of the sauna. Always check the fine print on booking websites to avoid surprises when checking out.

Recommended Booking Websites for Tromsø

Booking.com: One of the most popular global platforms, it offers a wide range of hotels, lodges, and unique accommodations. Filters allow you to sort by price, guest rating, or proximity to popular landmarks.

Hotels.com: Another reliable platform, known for offering reward nights. You earn one free night for every 10 booked, which could be useful if Tromsø is part of a larger Norwegian itinerary.

Expedia: With a vast selection of hotels, car rentals, and bundled deals, Expedia is useful for package bookings that might include flights or activities like Northern Lights tours.

Scandic Hotels Website: Scandic is a prominent hotel chain in Norway. By booking directly through their site, you often receive exclusive deals or additional perks not available on third-party platforms.

Nordic Choice Hotels: Similar to Scandic, this chain is well-known in the Nordic region, and booking directly through their website often provides better flexibility, loyalty points, or extra services.

Chapter 3

Must-Visit Attractions

Northern Lights

There are few things in life that stir the soul quite like witnessing the Northern Lights. It's not just a visual spectacle; it's an experience that touches something deeper, something primal. The moment those first glimmers of green start to ripple across the Arctic sky, you realize you're witnessing one of nature's most magical performances, and nothing quite prepares you for it.

Seeing the Northern Lights in Tromsø is an experience unlike any other. Located deep within the Arctic Circle, Tromsø offers one of the best chances to see the aurora borealis, and the city itself feels like it's been placed here for this very reason. The long winter nights, stretching for months, provide ample opportunity to catch this elusive phenomenon. But it's not just about catching a glimpse; it's about the entire journey to get there, the anticipation that builds as the sun sets, and the sky darkens.

When you first arrive in Tromsø, you might be filled with excitement, hoping the lights will show themselves on your very first night. But there's an element of patience that comes with the Northern Lights—there are no guarantees, and that's part of the magic. It's not a show that can be scheduled. It's something you have to wait for, and when it does happen, it feels like a gift from the universe. The wait is often spent in awe of the Arctic night itself. Stepping outside of the city, away from the streetlights and into the dark, silent wilderness, you feel small in the vastness of it all. The stars, brighter than you've ever seen them, seem to blanket the entire sky. The air is crisp, the kind of cold that bites at your cheeks, but it also feels refreshing—an awakening of the senses. The snow under your boots crunches as you find a spot to stand still, your eyes scanning the sky, hoping for that first shimmer of light.

Then, just when you think the sky couldn't be more peaceful, it begins. At first, it might be subtle—a faint greenish glow on the horizon, almost like a whisper. But soon, that glow starts to grow, to shift and dance. It's mesmerizing. You watch as the green turns brighter, then stretches out, swirling across the sky in waves. Sometimes, hints of pink or purple weave their way into the display, adding depth and mystery to the performance above. It's a dance that feels both delicate and powerful, a reminder of the beauty and unpredictability of nature.

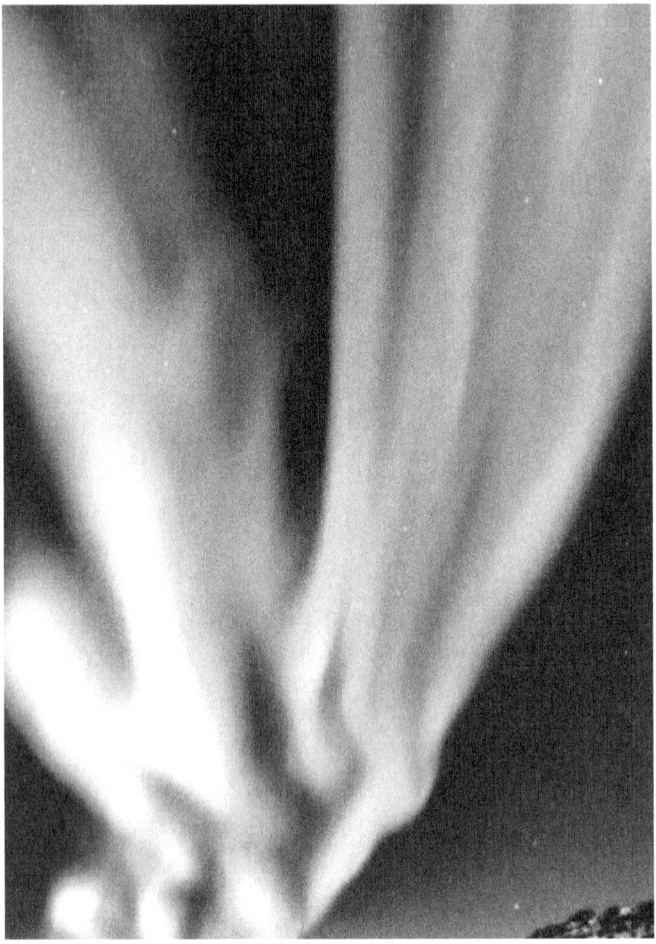

It's also deeply personal. The lights may show themselves to many people at once, but how they touch you is unique. For some, it's a spiritual moment—a connection to something bigger than themselves. For others, it's a sense of fulfillment, checking off a long-held dream from their bucket list. But for everyone, it's unforgettable. After the lights begin to fade and the sky returns to its starry stillness, there's a sense of calm that washes over you. Visiting Tromsø isn't just about seeing the Northern Lights; it's about feeling them. It's about standing beneath that Arctic sky and being reminded of the world's natural beauty, its mysteries, and the joy of witnessing something so spectacular. The Northern Lights aren't just an attraction, they're an invitation to slow down, to look up, and to be present in a way that few experiences can offer.

Arctic Cathedral

As you approach Tromsø, standing tall against the backdrop of Arctic mountains, the Arctic Cathedral immediately captures your attention. Its stark, angular silhouette stands out against the snowy landscape, an architectural marvel that feels as though it belongs to the very mountains it mirrors. This isn't just a building—it's a statement. A bold, modern structure that both complements and contrasts the rugged, ancient landscape of northern Norway.

The Arctic Cathedral, or **"Ishavskatedralen"** as it's known locally, was completed in 1965 and has since become one of Tromsø's most iconic landmarks. Walking up to it, you can't help but feel drawn to its striking design. The crisp white walls, constructed from concrete, rise sharply into the sky like a series of triangular peaks. These geometric forms evoke the natural beauty of the surrounding region—the mountains, the glaciers, the sharpness of the Arctic environment. In a place as wild as Tromsø, this cathedral seems to hold its own, standing proud and resolute. But it's not just the exterior that makes the Arctic Cathedral so special. Step inside, and you'll feel an immediate sense of peace and calm wash over you. The walls, pure white and minimalist, reflect the simplicity and purity of the Arctic itself. Light floods the interior, especially during the long summer days, giving the space an ethereal quality. It's not overwhelming or grand in the traditional sense, but there's something deeply spiritual about the atmosphere. The silence feels profound, as if the very space is inviting you to pause, to reflect, to find a moment of stillness in an otherwise fast-paced world.

The main attraction within the cathedral is its stunning stained glass window, which stands at the back of the building like a beacon of color and light. Designed by Norwegian artist Victor Sparre, the window stretches nearly the full height of the cathedral and depicts a dramatic scene of Christ with outstretched arms, surrounded by vibrant shades of blue, yellow, and red. The artistry here is breathtaking. The way the light filters through the glass creates a dynamic play of colors, casting soft, shifting hues onto the stark white walls. The effect is mesmerizing, as though the entire building is breathing, alive with the changing light. It's easy to feel a sense of reverence here, even if you're not religious. The Arctic Cathedral transcends its function as a place of worship—it feels like a tribute to nature itself. There's an undeniable connection between the building and the environment, a symbiosis that makes it feel as though the cathedral is a natural part of the landscape. The sharp, angular lines of the architecture echo the jagged mountains, and the play of light and shadow inside mirrors the dramatic contrasts of the Arctic's ever-changing seasons.

Visitors often speak of the feeling of awe when attending one of the cathedral's midnight concerts. Imagine sitting in the quiet of the night, surrounded by the soft glow of candlelight, as the music fills the space with hauntingly beautiful melodies. Even if you visit during the day, that sense of magic remains. The Arctic Cathedral stands as a reminder of how human creativity and nature can come together to create something truly special. It's not just a place to visit, but a place to feel. A place that inspires quiet contemplation, even for those just passing through. And as you walk away from the cathedral, with its triangular form fading into the distance, you can't help but carry a piece of it with you. That feeling of standing on the edge of the Arctic world, where modern design and ancient nature meet, stays with you long after you've left Tromsø.

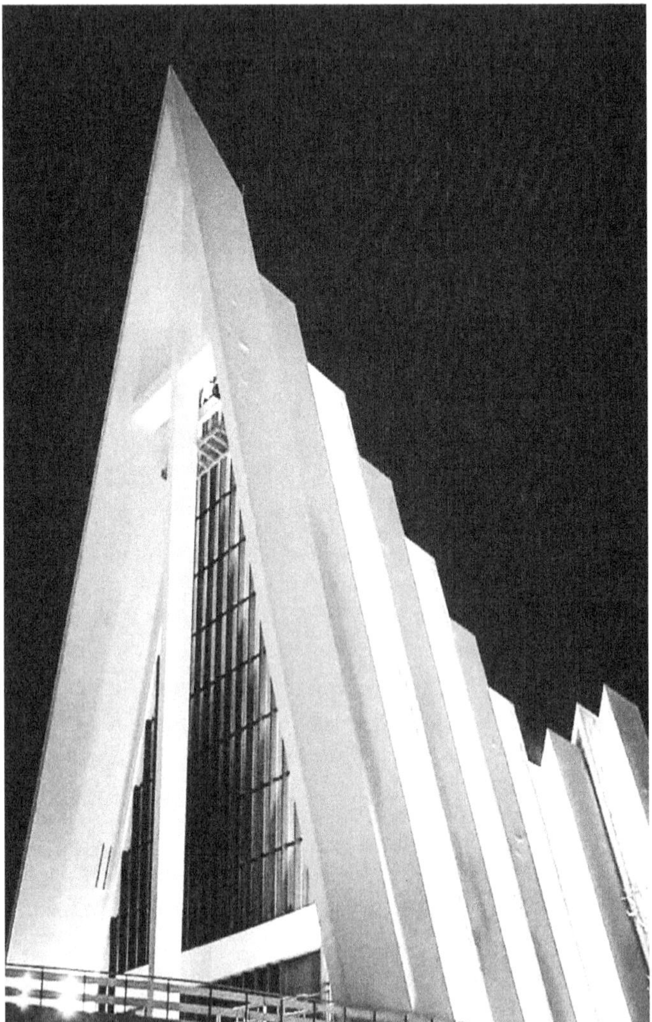

Polaria Aquarium

Stepping into Polaria Aquarium is like stepping into a story about survival, beauty, and the fragile balance of life in the Arctic. From the moment you see the building, its design mimicking blocks of ice shoved ashore. It's not just another tourist attraction, Polaria feels like an invitation, an invitation to dive deeper into the icy world that's so often spoken about but rarely understood.

As you enter, the cool air wraps around you, almost as if the Arctic itself is breathing down your neck. You walk in, and it's not the noise of crowds or chatter that hits you, but this quiet sense of awe. Then, you catch a glimpse of the stars of the show: the bearded seals. In a way that's hard to explain, watching them swim is calming, almost therapeutic. They glide so effortlessly through the water, with their wide, expressive eyes following you as you move around the tank. There's this playful nature to them—they're curious, but in a way that makes you feel like they're just as interested in you as you are in them.

Standing there, with only the glass between you and these Arctic creatures, it's hard not to feel a connection. You begin to wonder about their lives out in the wild—the cold they must endure, the miles of frozen ocean they call home. And yet, here they are, floating and twisting with such grace, completely at ease in an environment that most of us could never survive. You can't help but admire their resilience.

But Polaria isn't just about the animals. It's about the Arctic itself—the harsh, beautiful, breathtaking Arctic. Then, there's the panoramic cinema. You sit down, the lights dim, and suddenly you're transported into the heart of the Arctic wilderness. It's impossible to describe the emotional pull of watching glaciers move, the Northern Lights dance across the sky, or the sea ice slowly breaking apart. As you walk out, back into the brisk Tromsø air, there's a mix of emotions. There's awe, a sense of wonder at the beauty you've just witnessed, but also a deep, lingering responsibility. The Arctic may seem distant, but Polaria makes it personal. You can't help but feel a connection to this icy world, and more importantly, a desire to protect it.

Polaria isn't just a place to visit. It's a place to feel the beauty, the fragility, and the urgency of the Arctic. And as you leave, you carry that feeling with you, long after the seals have slipped from view and the icy cold has faded into memory.

Tromsø Kunstforening

Tromsø Kunstforening feels like finding a hidden refuge in the midst of the Arctic chill. As you enter, the warmth of the gallery wraps around you, offering a stark contrast to the cold Tromsø streets you just left behind. It's as if you've discovered a cozy corner where creativity and community converge, creating a space brimming with life and emotion. The gallery's charm is immediately apparent. Its intimate setting invites you to take a deep breath and immerse yourself in the art. Each exhibit seems to pulse with the energy and passion of its creator. As you walk through the rooms, you're greeted by a dynamic array of artworks that range from striking contemporary pieces to subtle, thought-provoking installations. There's a feeling of quiet anticipation in the air, as if the art is waiting for you to connect with it on a personal level. The lighting within the gallery is soft yet purposeful, casting gentle shadows that bring out the depth and texture of each piece. It's as if the space itself is in conversation with the art, highlighting its unique qualities and inviting you to linger. You might find yourself drawn into a painting's intricate details or mesmerized by the elegance of a sculpture. There's a profound sense of connection as you experience the art, feeling the emotions and stories that each piece conveys.

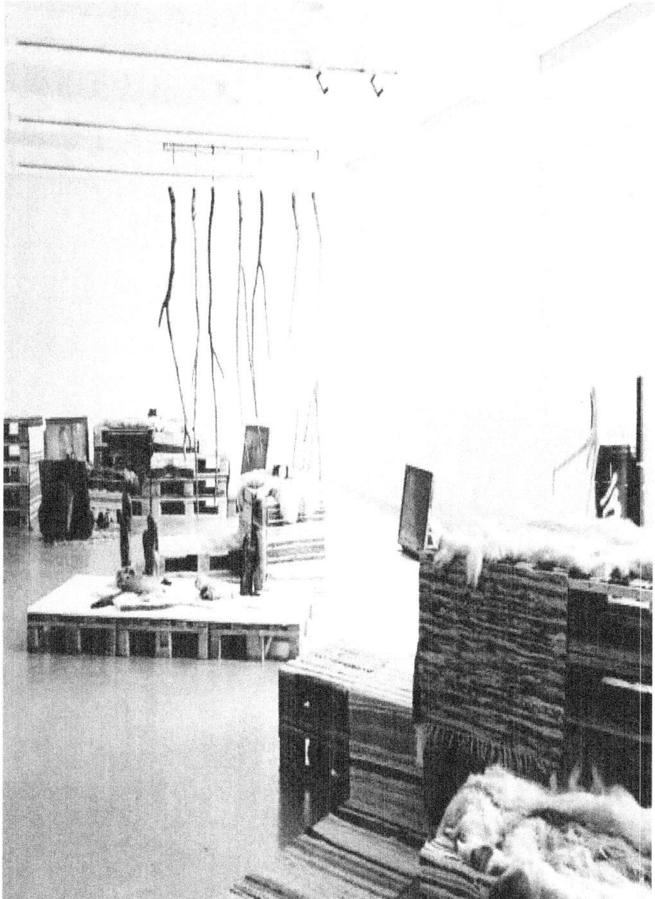

What sets Tromsø Kunstforening apart is its dedication to showcasing local and Nordic artists. The art here is not just visually stunning; it resonates with the essence of the Arctic. You can sense the artists' deep connection to the land and its people, their work reflecting the raw beauty and stark realities of life in this remote region. The gallery's staff add another layer of warmth to your visit. Their genuine enthusiasm and love for the art are palpable. They're eager to share their knowledge and insights, and their personal stories about the artists and their work enhance your understanding and appreciation. It's clear that they view Tromsø Kunstforening as more than just an exhibition space; it's a living, breathing part of the community where art and people come together. As you leave Tromsø Kunstforening, there's a sense of contentment that lingers. The gallery has offered you not just a glimpse into the Arctic's artistic soul but a heartfelt connection to its vibrant creative community. It's a place where the cold meets the warmth of human expression, leaving you with a deeper appreciation for the art, the artists, and the unique spirit of Tromsø.

Tromsø Domkirke

Tromsø Domkirke stands gracefully in the heart of Tromsø, a warm, inviting presence amid the chilly Arctic air. Its simple, white wooden facade seems almost to glow with a quiet dignity, offering a gentle welcome to all who approach. This cathedral, the northernmost of its kind in the world, has been a steadfast witness to the lives and stories of Tromsø's people since it was completed in 1861. Entering Tromsø Domkirke, you immediately feel a shift from the brisk, crisp Arctic world outside to a space of calm and reflection. The interior is bathed in a soft, natural light that filters through beautiful stained glass windows, casting a serene glow across the wooden pews. There's a sense of peace here that's both soothing and uplifting, inviting you to pause and breathe in the tranquility. The warmth of the church's wooden interior creates an atmosphere of intimacy and comfort. The high, gently arching ceilings and the intricately carved details in the woodwork add a touch of elegance without overwhelming the space. It's as though the church has been designed not just as a place of worship, but as a gathering spot for the community—a place where people come together, not just to pray, but to connect and share in life's moments.

You might find yourself drawn to the subtle beauty of the church's features, the smooth, worn wooden pews that have seen generations of worshippers, the softly glowing chandeliers that light up the space with a warm, inviting light. Each detail, from the delicate carvings on the altar to the lovingly preserved historical artifacts, tells a story of devotion and care.

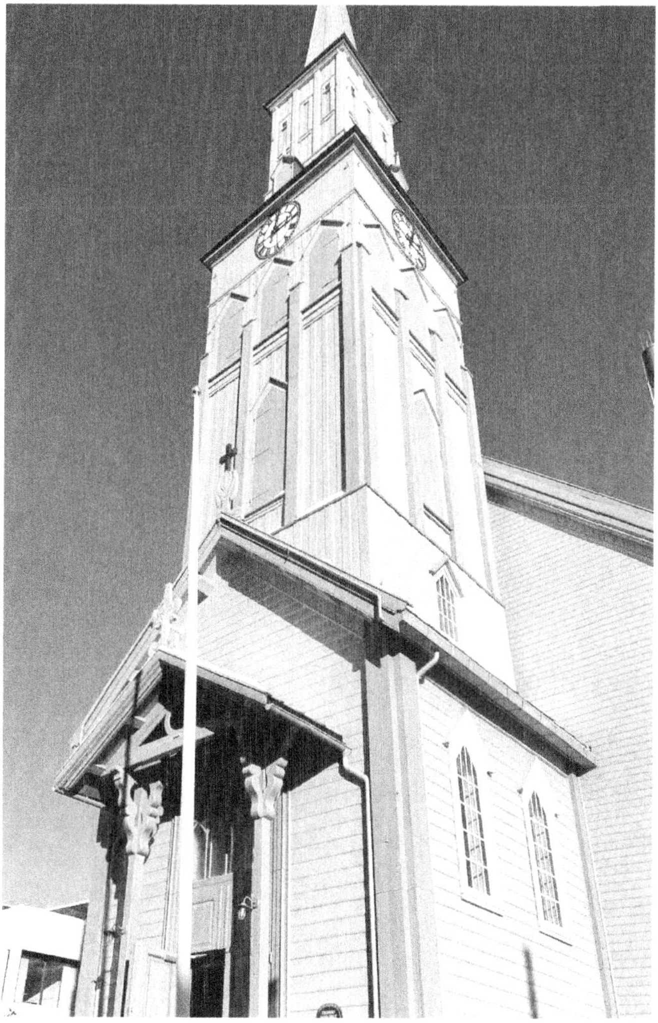

Tromsø Domkirke is more than just a historical landmark; it's a living, vibrant part of the community. It's a place where life happens—where weddings are celebrated, christenings take place, and where people come together to find solace and joy. If you're lucky enough to visit during a service or a special event, you'll experience firsthand the sense of unity and connection that fills the church. The sound of hymns sung by the congregation, the gentle rustle of programs, and the shared smiles of those gathered create a feeling of togetherness that's deeply moving.

As you leave Tromsø Domkirke, you carry with you a sense of serenity and connection. The church's blend of history, simplicity, and community warmth leaves a lasting impression. It's more than just a visit to a historic site—it's an encounter with a place that embodies the spirit of Tromsø, offering a moment of reflection and a reminder of the enduring bonds that unite people, both past and present.

Arctic-Alpine Botanic Gardens

The gardens unfold before you as a testament to the remarkable resilience and beauty of plant life that thrives in one of the harshest climates on Earth. The garden's entrance, with its subtle hints of what lies ahead, feels like a gentle invitation into a world where nature's creativity and endurance are on full display. Once inside, the stark contrast between the vibrant, colorful plant life and the rugged, rocky surroundings strikes a deep chord. You find yourself surrounded by a tapestry of delicate alpine flowers, resilient shrubs, and hardy lichens, all thriving in a landscape that seems both harsh and nurturing.

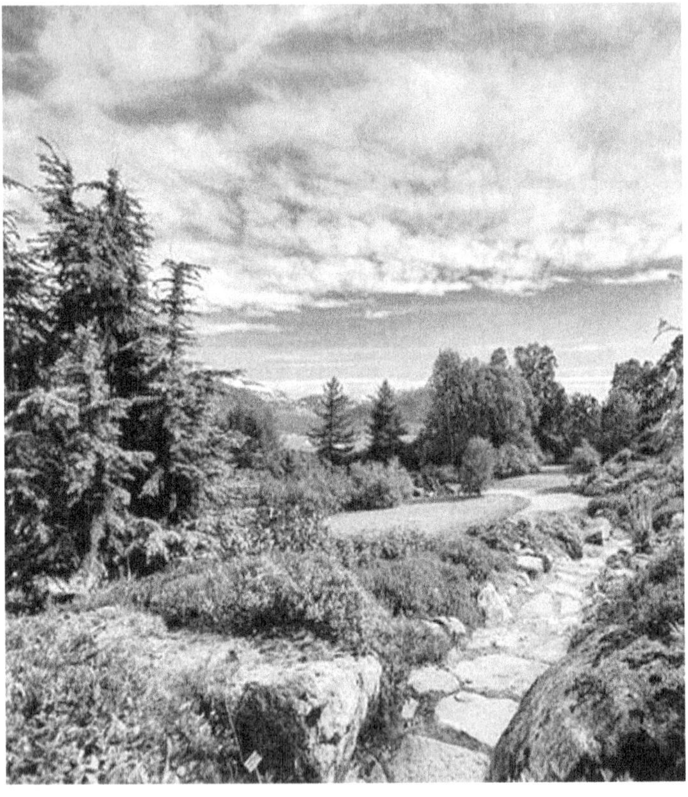

There's something profoundly moving about wandering through the garden's winding paths. The air is crisp and refreshing, carrying with it the faint, sweet aroma of blooming plants. Each step brings a new discovery—a patch of bright Arctic poppies, a cluster of soft, green mosses, or a splash of color from a hardy alpine bloom. The beauty of these plants, so perfectly adapted to their environment, evokes a sense of awe and appreciation for the intricate balance of nature.

What really touches the heart is the way the garden reflects the delicate relationship between nature and human care. The meticulous attention to detail, from the carefully arranged garden beds to the informative displays, speaks to a deep respect for the plants and their remarkable adaptations. It's clear that every aspect of the garden has been thoughtfully designed to showcase the resilience and beauty of these Arctic and alpine species.

As you explore, there's a feeling of peaceful reflection. The garden offers a chance to connect with the natural world in a deeply personal way. You might find yourself pausing to admire the intricate patterns of a flowering plant or the subtle beauty of a moss-covered rock. It's a reminder that even in the most challenging environments, life finds a way to flourish, and beauty emerges from the most unexpected places.

The educational elements of the garden add another layer of richness to your visit. Informative signs and displays provide insights into the unique adaptations of the plants, allowing you to appreciate their incredible ability to thrive in extreme conditions. This blend of beauty and knowledge creates an experience that is both enlightening and emotionally resonant.

Leaving the Arctic-Alpine Botanic Gardens, you carry with you a renewed sense of wonder and connection. The garden's blend of natural beauty and human care leaves a lasting impression, reminding you of the extraordinary resilience of life in the Arctic. It's more than just a botanical garden; it's a celebration of nature's triumphs and a poignant reminder of the delicate, enduring beauty that exists even in the harshest climates.

Tromsø Catholic Church

Tromsø Catholic Church, known locally as St. Joseph's Church, is a place where tranquility and reflection blend seamlessly with a rich tapestry of history and community spirit. As you approach this inviting sanctuary, its charming, modest exterior stands as a quiet beacon of peace amidst the bustling life of Tromsø. The moment you step inside, you're enveloped by a warm, serene atmosphere. The soft glow of light filtering through stained glass windows casts gentle hues across the interior, creating a sense of calm and welcome. The space is thoughtfully designed, with its simple wooden pews and elegant altar exuding a sense of reverence and tranquility.

This church is more than just a place of worship; it's a haven where the community comes together. The intimate setting fosters a deep connection among those who gather here, whether for a quiet moment of prayer or a lively community event. You can almost feel the collective warmth of the people who have walked these aisles, sharing in life's joys and sorrows, finding solace and celebration in this sacred space.

The church's history adds another layer of depth to your visit. Established in 1939, Tromsø Catholic Church has been a steadfast presence for the local Catholic community through decades of change. Its architectural style reflects both traditional and modern influences, mirroring the way the church has grown and evolved with its community over time. The blend of past and present creates a unique atmosphere, where history and modern life intersect in a meaningful way. The serene beauty of the church's interior invites contemplation. As you sit quietly, you might find yourself reflecting on the stories and lives that have intersected in this space. The church's modest but elegant design encourages a deep sense of peace and connection, allowing you to experience a moment of calm away from the hustle of everyday life.

What's truly special about Tromsø Catholic Church is its role as a community cornerstone. Beyond its function as a place of worship, it serves as a gathering spot for various events, from social gatherings to charity drives. This sense of community spirit is palpable, and you can feel the warmth and dedication of the people who are part of this vibrant congregation. Visiting Tromsø Catholic Church is more than just a sightseeing stop; it's an opportunity to connect with the essence of Tromsø's community and history. The church offers a peaceful retreat and a reminder of the ways in which faith and fellowship can create a sense of belonging and solace.

Chapter 4

Outdoor Activities

Hiking and Trekking in Tromsø

As you begin your hike up Mount Fløya, the city of Tromsø slowly recedes behind you. With each step, you're enveloped in the stillness of the Arctic wilderness. The climb is challenging, but there's a profound joy in feeling your heart race as you push your limits. When you finally reach the summit, the world below seems to unfold in an endless expanse of beauty. The view is breathtaking, a sprawling canvas of islands and fjords, and it's impossible not to feel a sense of triumph and connection with the earth. On gentler trails, like those around Lake Prestvannet, the experience is soothing and reflective. As you stroll along the lake's edge, you're surrounded by the soft whisper of nature. The water's surface mirrors the surrounding mountains in a tranquil dance of colors. This serene setting invites you to slow down and savor the moment. The peacefulness here is palpable, offering a deep sense of relaxation and contentment.

Every hike in Tromsø is an opportunity to connect deeply with both nature and yourself. Whether you're tackling steep ascents or enjoying a leisurely walk, the feeling of being immersed in such pristine landscapes is profoundly moving. You might find yourself lost in thought, contemplating life as you navigate the trails. The sense of accomplishment that comes with reaching a summit or completing a trail is matched by the beauty of the journey itself.

Sharing these experiences with others adds another layer of richness. The camaraderie of fellow hikers, the shared smiles, and the stories exchanged along the way create a sense of community and warmth. These interactions, combined with the natural splendor surrounding you, make each hike a memorable experience. Hiking and trekking in Tromsø isn't just about covering miles—it's about feeling the Arctic wind on your face, breathing in the pure, fresh air, and embracing the raw, untouched beauty of the landscape. It's about finding joy in the challenge and peace in the stillness. Each step taken in this majestic setting brings a deeper appreciation for the world around you and the simple, profound pleasures of being in nature.

Dog sledding

Dog sledding in Tromsø is an experience that captivates the heart and invigorates the spirit.

Imagine the thrill of gliding through the snow-covered landscapes of the Arctic, surrounded by pristine wilderness, with the rhythmic sound of dog paws pounding the snow and the crisp, cold air brushing against your face. This isn't just an adventure; it's a deeply emotional journey that connects you with nature and the remarkable bond between humans and dogs. From the moment you arrive at the dog sledding base, there's an undeniable sense of excitement in the air.

As you meet your team of sled dogs, it's hard not to be touched by their sheer joy and eagerness. They seem to sense your anticipation and respond with boundless energy. Each dog has its own unique character, and spending time with them, patting their fur and feeling their warmth, creates an instant bond. Their excitement is contagious, making it easy to share in their enthusiasm.

When you finally hop onto the sled, there's a thrilling sense of anticipation. The moment the sled begins to move, you feel the rush of the cold air against your face and the exhilarating freedom of gliding through the snow. The landscape unfolds around you in a breathtaking panorama of white, with snow-covered trees and frozen lakes stretching out as far as the eye can see. The quiet of the Arctic is profound, broken only by the gentle, rhythmic swish of the sled and the joyful barks of the dogs.

As you travel deeper into the wilderness, the connection with the landscape deepens. The snow crunches softly beneath the sled, and the world feels both vast and intimate. You might catch glimpses of wildlife or marvel at the play of light on the snow, adding to the sense of wonder. Each turn and twist in the trail offers a new perspective, a fresh burst of beauty that keeps you captivated and engaged. There's a certain magic in the way the sled dogs move effortlessly through the snow, their teamwork and coordination a testament to their training and natural instincts. Watching them work in harmony is mesmerizing and deeply moving. Their dedication and strength highlight the incredible bond between human and dog, a relationship built on trust, mutual respect, and shared adventure.

The experience of dog sledding also brings moments of quiet reflection. As the sled glides smoothly across the snow, you have time to take in the vast, untouched beauty of the Arctic landscape. The serenity of the surroundings invites introspection, offering a rare opportunity to disconnect from everyday life and simply be present in the moment. The peacefulness of the snowy expanse, combined with the thrill of the ride, creates a profound sense of contentment and joy. The journey concludes with a sense of accomplishment and gratitude. Returning to the base, there's a feeling of having been part of something truly special—a unique adventure that blends the beauty of nature with the bond between humans and dogs. The warmth of the dogs and the shared experiences make the ending bittersweet, as you say goodbye to your canine companions and reflect on the adventure you've just experienced.

Snowmobiling

Snowmobiling in Tromsø is an exhilarating adventure that combines the thrill of speed with the stunning beauty of Arctic landscapes. Picture yourself starting a snowmobile, feeling the rumble of the engine beneath you, and setting off into a winter wonderland where the only limits are those of your imagination. The excitement begins the moment you gear up. The crisp, cold air is invigorating, and the anticipation of the adventure ahead is palpable. As you glide across the snow-covered terrain, you're immediately struck by the sensation of freedom. The snowmobile effortlessly cuts through the powdery snow, creating a sense of weightlessness and exhilaration.

The landscape around you is a breathtaking panorama of white, with snow-covered peaks and frozen lakes stretching as far as the eye can see. The serenity of the Arctic is contrasted by the exhilarating rush of the snowmobile. It's a thrilling experience that keeps you on your toes, as you navigate through a pristine winter landscape that feels both vast and intimate.

Snowmobiling in Tromsø offers a unique way to explore the Arctic wilderness. The speed and agility of the snowmobile allow you to cover ground quickly, taking in a variety of stunning views in a short amount of time. Whether you're speeding across open fields or maneuvering through winding trails, every moment is filled with a sense of adventure and discovery.

The feeling of the cold wind against your face, the roar of the engine, and the thrill of the ride create an exhilarating mix of sensations. As you zoom across the snow, you're surrounded by the pure, untouched beauty of the Arctic. Each twist and turn in the trail reveals new vistas, from dramatic mountain ranges to serene frozen lakes, all bathed in the soft light of the Arctic sun.

One of the most memorable aspects of snowmobiling in Tromsø is the opportunity to connect with the natural environment in a way that's both thrilling and respectful. The snowmobile allows you to access remote areas that are otherwise difficult to reach, giving you a chance to witness the unspoiled beauty of the Arctic. As you ride, you might catch sight of local wildlife or experience the subtle changes in the landscape, adding to the sense of wonder and adventure.

The experience is also enhanced by the camaraderie and shared excitement of being on a snowmobile tour. There's a special bond that forms among participants as you share the thrill of the ride and the joy of discovering the Arctic together. The guides, with their expertise and enthusiasm, add to the experience, providing insights into the landscape and ensuring that you make the most of your adventure.

As the tour comes to an end, there's a sense of exhilaration and satisfaction that lingers. The thrill of the ride, combined with the beauty of the Arctic surroundings, creates a powerful and memorable experience. Snowmobiling in Tromsø is not just about the speed and excitement; it's about connecting with the landscape, embracing the adventure, and creating lasting memories.

Snowmobiling in Tromsø offers a unique blend of thrill and beauty. It's an adventure that combines the joy of speed with the serene splendor of the Arctic. Every moment is filled with excitement, discovery, and a deep appreciation for the stunning landscapes that surround you.

Chapter 5

Cultural experience

Sami Culture and Reindeer Sledding

Experiencing Sami culture and reindeer sledding in Tromsø is like progressing into a world where ancient traditions and breathtaking landscapes come together in a harmony that's both captivating and humbling. This adventure isn't just about the thrill of the ride; it's about connecting with a rich heritage and feeling a deep sense of wonder and respect for a culture that has thrived in the Arctic for centuries. The journey begins with a warm welcome from the Sami people, whose hospitality is as genuine as their traditions. As you arrive at the Sami camp, you're greeted with the sight of traditional lavvu tents, their conical shapes standing proudly against the snowy backdrop. Inside, the warmth and coziness of the fire provide a stark contrast to the cold outside, creating a welcoming atmosphere that instantly puts you at ease.

Listening to the Sami guides share their stories and traditions is a deeply moving experience. Their connection to the land and their way of life is profound, and their passion for preserving their culture is palpable. As they recount tales of their ancestors and the natural world, you can feel the weight of history and the pride they take in their heritage. As you step into the sled, the excitement of the ride is matched by the sense of reverence for the animals that make it possible. Reindeer are at the heart of Sami life, and their role in this traditional mode of transportation is both practical and symbolic. The sight of these majestic creatures, with their graceful antlers and gentle demeanor, is awe-inspiring.

Once the sled is set in motion, you're enveloped in a serene, almost magical atmosphere. The rhythmic glide of the sled over the snow, accompanied by the soft pattern of reindeer hooves, creates a sense of tranquility and wonder. The Arctic landscape stretches out before you, a pristine canvas of white that seems to go on forever. As you travel through this breathtaking terrain, it's easy to feel a deep connection to the land and the traditions that have shaped it. The experience of reindeer sledding also provides a unique insight into the Sami way of life. The guides share their knowledge of how they use reindeer for transportation, clothing, and even food, illustrating the deep bond between the Sami people and their animals. It's a humbling reminder of how closely their lives are intertwined with the natural world, and how their traditions have evolved to sustain and celebrate this relationship.

There's a sense of reflection and appreciation for the journey you've just experienced after returning to the camp. The combination of the thrilling ride, the serene beauty of the landscape, and the rich cultural insights creates a powerful and memorable experience. Sharing stories and enjoying a traditional Sami meal around the fire, you feel a sense of connection not just to the people you've met, but to the timeless traditions that have been passed down through generations.

Tromsø International Film Festival

The Tromsø International Film Festival is more than just a series of movie screenings; it's a vibrant celebration of storytelling, creativity, and the power of cinema. Held in the heart of Arctic Norway, this festival transforms the city into a cultural hub where the magic of film meets the wonder of the polar landscape. From the moment you arrive at the festival, there's an undeniable buzz in the air. The excitement is palpable as filmmakers, enthusiasts, and locals come together, united by their love for cinema. The festival's unique setting against the backdrop of snowy streets and the Northern Lights creates an atmosphere that's both electric and intimate. It's as if the Arctic itself becomes a part of the film experience, adding an extra layer of enchantment to the event.

Walking into the festival venues, you're immediately struck by the sense of community and camaraderie. The theaters are filled with people eagerly discussing their favorite films, sharing recommendations, and forming new connections. There's a feeling of collective enthusiasm, as everyone is here to celebrate the art of storytelling and explore new perspectives. The festival's setting fosters a sense of closeness and shared experience, making it easy to strike up conversations and immerse yourself in the world of film.

Each screening is a journey in itself. The films showcased at the Tromsø International Film Festival are as diverse as the audience they attract. From thought-provoking documentaries to innovative experimental films and heartwarming narratives, the festival offers something for everyone. The selection is a reflection of the festival's commitment to showcasing both emerging talent and established voices, creating a rich tapestry of cinematic experiences. One of the most touching aspects of the festival is the opportunity to hear from the filmmakers themselves. During Q&A sessions and panel discussions, directors, writers, and actors share their insights and experiences, offering a behind-the-scenes look at the creative process. These interactions provide a deeper understanding of the films and allow you to connect with the stories and the people behind them on a more personal level.

The festival is also a celebration of the Arctic's unique beauty. As you move between screenings and events, you're treated to breathtaking views of the surrounding landscape. The contrast between the warm glow of the theater and the crisp, cold air outside adds a magical touch to the experience. It's a reminder of the special atmosphere that Tromsø offers—a place where the stark beauty of winter and the warmth of cultural events coexist in perfect harmony.

In addition to the films, the Tromsø International Film Festival features a range of events and activities that enhance the overall experience. Workshops, networking sessions, and social gatherings provide opportunities to dive deeper into the world of cinema and connect with fellow film lovers. These moments of interaction are often just as memorable as the films themselves, creating lasting bonds and fostering a sense of community among attendees.

The films, conversations, and experiences shared over the course of the event leave a lasting impact. You leave with a renewed appreciation for the power of storytelling and a collection of new perspectives and connections that will stay with you long after the festival has ended.

The Tromsø International Film Festival is a celebration of cinema in one of the most enchanting settings imaginable. It's an event that captures the essence of what makes film so powerful—theability

to connect people, inspire conversations, and transport us to different worlds. Whether you're a seasoned film buff or a curious newcomer, the festival offers an unforgettable experience that celebrates the art of storytelling and the beauty of the Arctic landscape.

Chapter 6

dining and culinary

Local Delicacies

Exploring local delicacies in Tromsø is like taking a journey through the heart of Arctic flavors. From hearty, warming fare to delicate, unique flavors, Tromsø's culinary scene offers a taste of the Arctic that's as unforgettable as the landscapes themselves.

When you first step into a local eatery or traditional restaurant in Tromsø, you're greeted by an inviting aroma that hints at the rich flavors to come. The emphasis here is on fresh, locally sourced ingredients that reflect the rugged beauty of the Arctic environment. Tromsø's cuisine often centers around ingredients that are both sustenance and celebration, embodying the spirit of the region's people and their connection to the land.

One of the most iconic local delicacies is **rakfisk,** a traditional fermented fish dish that is both an acquired taste and a beloved part of Norwegian culinary tradition. The process of fermenting trout or salmon for several months creates a unique, tangy flavor that pairs perfectly with traditional accompaniments like sour cream, onions, and flatbread. Sampling rakfisk is a rite of passage for those keen to experience authentic Arctic cuisine, and the dish's deep, earthy flavors offer a glimpse into the region's food heritage.

Another must-try is **reindeer stew,** a dish that's both comforting and richly flavorful. Reindeer meat, tender and savory, is slow-cooked with root vegetables, juniper berries, and a blend of aromatic herbs. The result is a hearty stew that warms you from the inside out, reflecting the hearty nature of traditional Sami fare. Eating reindeer stew is not just about savoring a meal; it's about connecting with the traditions of the Sami people, who have relied on reindeer as a vital part of their diet for centuries.

For a lighter, yet equally intriguing taste, consider trying **klippfisk, dried and salted cod** that has been a staple in Scandinavian cuisine for generations. The cod is rehydrated and used in various dishes, from stews to casseroles, and offers a deep, concentrated flavor that's both salty and satisfying. This dish is a testament to the region's history of preservation methods and the ways in which local people have adapted to the Arctic environment.

Arctic char is another local favorite, a fish native to the cold waters of the Arctic. It's often prepared simply, allowing the delicate, slightly sweet flavor of the fish to shine. Whether grilled, smoked, or served as a pâté, Arctic char is a true delicacy that

147

reflects the pristine waters and unspoiled natural beauty of the region.

Don't miss out on sampling cloudberries, a small but mighty fruit that thrives in the Arctic tundra. Cloudberries are often used in desserts, jams, and sauces, offering a unique blend of tart and sweet flavors. Their vibrant orange color and distinctive taste make them a standout ingredient in Arctic cuisine, and enjoying them in a local dessert is a delightful way to end your meal.

Best Restaurants in Tromsø

Tromsø's culinary scene is a reflection of its stunning Arctic surroundings, blending traditional Norwegian flavors with contemporary flair. Dining here isn't just about eating; it's about experiencing a heartfelt connection to the land and its people through food. Each restaurant offers a unique window into Tromsø's vibrant food culture, where you can savor local delicacies and innovative creations in settings that are as inviting as the meals themselves.

1. Emma's Drømmekjøkken

Emma's Drømmekjøkken feels like a warm embrace on a cold Arctic day. This delightful bistro is esteemed for its intimate atmosphere and beautifully presented dishes. The menu highlights local ingredients, with options ranging from reindeer steak to Arctic char. Emma's is a place where traditional Norwegian comfort food meets modern sophistication, making it a perfect spot for a memorable meal.

2. Fiskekompaniet

For seafood lovers, Fiskekompaniet is a culinary gem. Located by the waterfront, this restaurant offers breathtaking views along with its fresh, high-quality seafood. The menu features a variety of dishes, including succulent shrimp, delicate cod, and the renowned fish soup. The restaurant's emphasis on freshness and flavor makes it a must-visit for anyone looking to experience Tromsø's maritime bounty.

3. Mathallen Tromsø

Mathallen Tromsø is a celebration of local produce and creativity. This vibrant eatery prides itself on using seasonal, locally sourced ingredients to craft dishes that are both inventive and deeply satisfying. From hearty meat dishes to fresh salads and unique desserts, Mathallen offers a diverse menu that reflects the best of Tromsø's food scene.

Their tasting menu is a great way to sample a range of flavors and experience the restaurant's culinary vision.

4. Bardus Bistro

Bardus Bistro combines a relaxed ambiance with a menu that showcases both traditional Norwegian dishes and international influences. The bistro is known for its creative use of local ingredients, resulting in dishes that are both flavorful and comforting. The warm, inviting atmosphere makes it an excellent choice for a casual meal or a special occasion.

5. Restaurant Smak

Restaurant Smak offers a refined dining experience with a focus on seasonal ingredients and innovative cooking techniques. The restaurant's elegant setting and attentive service create an atmosphere of sophistication and comfort. Each dish is a work of art, combining local flavors with a touch of culinary flair. The tasting menu is highly recommended for a full exploration of Smak's culinary offerings.

6. Hildr Gastro Bar

Hildr Gastro Bar is where Tromsø's food scene comes alive with energy and creativity. This lively spot serves up a range of dishes that blend traditional Norwegian flavors with contemporary twists. The menu is designed for sharing, making it a great place to enjoy a meal with friends or family in a relaxed, social setting. Their small plates are perfect for sampling a variety of flavors.

7. Polar Restaurant

Polar Restaurant is a culinary haven that celebrates Tromsø's rich food heritage. The menu features classic Norwegian dishes made with locally sourced ingredients, prepared with a modern touch. The restaurant's warm, welcoming atmosphere and commitment to quality make it a favorite among both locals and visitors.

Chapter 7

shopping and souvenir

Local Market

The market's lively atmosphere is contagious. The air is filled with the enticing aroma of freshly baked bread and traditional Norwegian treats. As you walk past stalls, the smell of krumkake—a delicate, waffle-like cookie—and lefse, a soft flatbread, invites you to sample and savor these local delights. Each bite of these pastries connects you to the rich culinary traditions of the region, offering a taste of Tromsø's comforting and hearty cuisine. The stalls are a treasure chest of unique finds. Here, you'll discover beautifully crafted woolen goods, from snug scarves to cozy sweaters. These items aren't just practical for the cold Arctic climate; they're imbued with the patterns and colors inspired by Tromsø's breathtaking landscapes. Each piece is a testament to the skill of local artisans who weave their passion and creativity into every stitch.

Wooden crafts are another highlight of the market. Hand-carved items, from intricate figurines to functional decor pieces, reflect the natural beauty and cultural heritage of Tromsø. These wooden treasures carry with them the essence of the region, turning each purchase into a meaningful keepsake. Imagine taking home a carved figure inspired by the Arctic wilderness or a beautifully crafted wooden bowl that echoes the tranquility of the northern fjords.

For those looking for edible souvenirs, the market is brimming with local specialties. Freshly caught fish, like dried cod, and jars of tangy cloudberry jam are perfect for bringing a taste of Tromsø back with you. These items offer a delicious way to remember your trip, allowing you to savor the flavors of the Arctic long after you've returned home.

The heart of the market experience lies in the interactions with the vendors. Their genuine smiles and passionate stories about their crafts and products add a personal touch to your visit. As they share the histories and traditions behind their goods, you feel a deeper connection to Tromsø. It's as if each purchase is not just a transaction but a shared experience, a moment of connection between you and the people who make this city so special.

Each item you choose carries a piece of Tromsø's warmth and creativity, making your memories of the city even more meaningful. As you leave the market with your treasures, you carry with you not just unique finds but also the heartfelt spirit of

Tromsø, making your experience truly unforgettable.

Boutique Stores

The moment you enter these boutiques, you're welcome by a warm, inviting atmosphere that feels almost like a friendly embrace. The soft lighting and artfully arranged displays make each visit feel personal, as if you're exploring someone's lovingly curated collection. The ambiance isn't just about aesthetics; it's about creating a space where every item tells a story and every purchase feels meaningful.

As you browse through racks of clothing, you'll notice how each piece seems to capture the spirit of Tromsø. There's a certain magic in a scarf that echoes the colors of the Northern Lights or a coat that combines sleek design with cozy warmth. These aren't just clothes, they're crafted expressions of the city's natural beauty and creativity.

Jewelry enthusiasts will be enchanted by the delicate pieces that showcase local materials like reindeer antler and Arctic stones. Each piece feels like a little piece of Tromsø's rugged landscape and shimmering skies, making them not just accessories but cherished mementos of your journey. The craftsmanship is evident in every detail, adding a personal touch that makes each item feel special.

The home decor items you'll find in Tromsø's boutiques are equally captivating. Imagine decorating your space with hand-woven textiles that bring a touch of Arctic elegance or displaying ceramics that reflect the region's artistic spirit. These aren't just decor items; they're little bits of Tromsø's charm that you can carry with you, turning your home into a haven of Arctic warmth.

The interactions with local shopkeepers are one of the highlights of the boutique experience. Their genuine enthusiasm and deep connection to their products infuse your shopping with a sense of intimacy. They're not just selling items; they're sharing their passion for Tromsø's culture and artistry. Listening to their stories and recommendations adds a personal layer to your purchases, making them feel even more special.

Shopping in Tromsø's boutiques isn't just about finding unique items; it's about connecting with the city's heart. Each item you choose carries a piece of Tromsø's spirit, reflecting its warmth, creativity, and natural beauty. The experience leaves you with more than just souvenirs. it offers a tangible connection to the city's soul, making your memories of Tromsø even more precious.

As you leave these charming boutiques, you'll feel a sense of having discovered something truly special. The pieces you take home are not just reminders of your trip but little fragments of Tromsø's essence, carrying with them the warmth and artistry that make the city unforgettable.

Chapter 8

Practical information tips

Currency and Payment in Tromsø

Navigating currency and payment in Tromsø is a breeze, letting you focus on soaking up the Arctic charm rather than stressing over money matters. Here's a warm and friendly guide to ensure your financial transactions are as smooth as the Northern Lights.

Currency

When you're in Tromsø, you'll be using the Norwegian Krone (NOK), symbolized by "kr." This currency is not just about numbers; it's a part of Norway's rich heritage. Imagine the crisp feel of the banknotes and the satisfying clink of the coins. Each piece of currency carries a story of the land you're exploring. The Krone is divided into 100 øre, and you'll find notes in denominations of 50, 100, 200, 500, and 1000 Krone, alongside coins in 1, 5, and 10 Krone, and 1 and 5 øre. Handling this money connects you with the local culture in a tangible way.

Exchanging Money

Finding places to exchange your home currency is easy and convenient. You can head to banks or exchange bureaus located throughout Tromsø, particularly in the city center and near the airport. The process is straightforward, and you'll be greeted with a friendly smile as you swap your currency for Krone. Many hotels also offer currency

161

exchange services, adding a touch of convenience to your stay. It's like having a little piece of Tromsø right at your fingertips!

ATMs

ATMs are scattered around Tromsø like little beacons of convenience. From the bustling city center to quieter corners, you'll find machines ready to dispense Norwegian Krone. These ATMs offer competitive exchange rates, letting you access cash with ease. Before you use one, check with your bank about any international fees—because, while the ATM might feel like a lifeline, unexpected charges are never a pleasant surprise.

Credit and Debit Cards

Credit and debit cards are your best friends in Tromsø. They're widely accepted, whether you're dining at a cozy café, staying at a charming hotel, or buying souvenirs. Visa and MasterCard are the go-to options, but don't worry if you have American Express or another card—most places are quite accommodating. The ease of swiping or tapping your card adds to the convenience of your Arctic adventure, allowing you to savor the moment without worrying about cash.

Mobile Payments

Embracing modern technology, many places in Tromsø accept mobile payments through apps like Apple Pay, Google Pay, and Vipps. These digital options make paying for your purchases feel almost magical. It's like having a high-tech, hassle-free way to manage your expenses, allowing you to glide through transactions with the touch of a screen.

Tipping

In Norway, tipping isn't a major tradition. Service charges are usually included in your bill, so there's no pressure to add extra. However, if you've been wowed by exceptional service and want to show your appreciation, a small tip or rounding up the bill is always a kind gesture. It's a way to share a smile and say thank you for making your experience memorable.

Budgeting Tips

As you enjoy Tromsø's stunning landscapes and unique experiences, keeping an eye on your budget can help you make the most of your trip. Here are a few heartfelt tips to keep your finances in check:

Plan Ahead: Research the costs of attractions, dining, and transport before you arrive. Knowing what to expect helps you budget more effectively, so you can focus on the fun.

Public Transport: Tromsø's public transport system is efficient and economical, making it a great way to get around and save money.

Local Cuisine: Delight in Tromsø's local food scene at charming cafes and restaurants. These spots often offer delicious meals at more reasonable prices than tourist-heavy establishments.

Language and Communication

Norwegian

Norwegian is the primary language spoken in Tromsø. With its melodic tones and unique expressions, Norwegian adds a special charm to the city's interactions. While you might not become fluent overnight, understanding a few key phrases can go a long way. Greetings like "Hei" (Hi) and "Takk" (Thank you) will be appreciated, and "Hvordan har du det?" (How are you?)

English: Your Friendly Companion

Don't worry if you're not familiar with Norwegian. English is widely spoken throughout Tromsø. Most locals speak English fluently. Whether you're ordering a meal, asking for directions, or chatting with hotel staff, you'll find that English serves as a reliable bridge. The ease of communication allows you to immerse yourself in Tromsø's experiences without language barriers.

Helpful Tips for Communication

To enhance your interactions and show respect for the local culture, consider these friendly tips:

Learn a Few Phrases: While English is commonly spoken, learning a few Norwegian phrases can endear you to the locals. Simple greetings and polite expressions go a long way in making connections and showing appreciation for the local culture.

Be Clear and Polite: When speaking English, clarity is key. Speak slowly and clearly, and don't hesitate to ask for repetition if you don't understand something. Politeness is universal, so a smile and a courteous tone will always be well-received.

Embrace Body Language: In addition to spoken words, body language plays a significant role in communication. A friendly smile, nodding, and making eye contact can help convey your message and create a warm atmosphere.

Use Translation Apps: If you're venturing off the beaten path or need assistance with more complex phrases, translation apps can be a helpful tool. They provide quick translations and help bridge any gaps in understanding.

Cultural Sensitivity

Being mindful of cultural norms enhances your experience in Tromsø. Norwegians are known for their reserved but friendly demeanor. Respect for personal space and a calm, polite approach are appreciated. Engaging in small talk and showing genuine interest in the local culture will make your interactions more meaningful.

Connecting with Locals

Engaging with Tromsø's residents can be one of the most rewarding aspects of your visit. Locals are generally welcoming and happy to share their city with you. Don't hesitate to ask for recommendations on where to eat, what to see, or how to experience Tromsø like a local. Your curiosity and enthusiasm will be met with warmth and helpful guidance.

Safety Tips and Emergency Contacts

Exploring Tromsø's breathtaking landscapes is an adventure filled with wonder. To ensure your trip remains as enjoyable and worry-free as possible, here are some essential safety tips and emergency contact information for your Arctic journey.

Safety Tips

- **Dress Appropriately**: Tromsø's weather can be extreme, especially in winter. Layering is key—wear thermal base layers, a waterproof outer layer, and insulated gloves, hats, and boots. Weather conditions can change rapidly, so being prepared will keep you comfortable and safe.
- **Be Weather-Wise**: Before heading out, check local weather forecasts. Tromsø's weather can shift quickly, and it's important to stay informed about conditions that might affect your plans, such as snowstorms or icy roads.
- **Travel in Groups**: If you're planning to explore the outdoors, such as hiking or snowmobiling, it's best to do so with others.

Solo ventures, especially in remote areas, can be risky due to the unpredictable Arctic weather and challenging terrain.

- **Follow Local Advice**: Pay attention to safety briefings and local advice, especially when engaging in activities like dog sledding or reindeer sledding. Guides and local operators provide valuable insights into safe practices and emergency procedures.
- **Stay Hydrated and Eat Well**: Even in cold weather, hydration and nutrition are important. Drink plenty of water and eat balanced meals to keep your energy levels up and avoid fatigue, which can affect your alertness and safety.
- **Stay Connected**: Keep your phone charged and have it with you at all times. Mobile reception is generally good in Tromsø, but if you're heading to more remote areas, a portable charger can be a lifesaver.

Emergency Contacts

- **Emergency Services**: For urgent assistance, dial 112. This number connects you to emergency services including police, fire, and medical help. It's essential to know this number in case of a serious emergency.
- **Police**: For non-urgent police matters or to report a crime, you can contact the local police station at +47 02800. The police are there to help with any issues you might encounter.
- **Medical Assistance**: For medical emergencies, you can reach the emergency room at the University Hospital of North Norway (UNN) by calling +47 77 62 80 00. The hospital is well-equipped to handle any medical needs you may have.
- **Road Safety**: If you need assistance on the road, whether it's for breakdowns or accidents, you can contact the Norwegian

Road Administration (Statens Vegvesen) at +47 22 07 30 00.

- **Tourist Information**: The Tromsø Tourist Information Center can be a helpful resource for general inquiries and assistance. They can be reached at +47 77 61 00 00 or visited at the center located in the heart of Tromsø.
- **Lost and Found**: If you lose something or find lost property, contact the Tromsø Police Department at +47 02800 or visit their office.

General Tips

- **Learn Basic Norwegian Phrases**: While English is widely spoken, knowing a few basic Norwegian phrases can be helpful in emergencies.
- **Keep a Map and Compass**: If you're exploring areas where GPS might not work,

a physical map and compass can be invaluable.

- **Inform Someone of Your Plans**: Let someone know your itinerary, especially if you're going on outdoor excursions or traveling to remote areas.

Steps to Scan The QR code

1. Open the Camera App

On most smartphones, the built-in camera app can scan QR codes. Open the camera app on your phone.

2. Point the Camera at the QR Code

Hold your phone steady and aim the camera at the QR code. Ensure the code fits within the camera frame.

3. Wait for the Notification

The phone will automatically detect the QR code. Once detected, a notification or link will appear at the top of your screen.

4. Tap the Notification

Tap the notification or link that appears to access the information stored in the QR code, whether it's a website, app, or other content.

5. Use a QR Code Scanner App (Optional)

If your phone's camera doesn't scan the code, download a QR code scanner app from your app store, open the app, and follow the same process.

This process allows you to quickly access any content linked to the QR code, such as websites, videos, or contact information.

7 Days itinerary for you

Day 1: Arrival and Exploration

- **Morning:** Arrive in Tromsø and settle into your hotel. If you have time, take a short walk around the town to get a feel for the place. Stay close to the city center for easy access to attractions.
- **Afternoon:** Visit the Arctic Cathedral, one of Tromsø's most iconic landmarks. Its stunning architecture and stained glass windows are worth admiring.
- **Evening:** Enjoy a leisurely dinner at Fiskekompaniet, a top-rated seafood restaurant. Taste local dishes like Arctic char or Norwegian salmon.

Day 2: Northern Lights and City Exploration

- **Morning:** Start with a visit to the Polaria Aquarium. Watch the fascinating seal show and learn more about the Arctic's unique ecosystem.
- **Afternoon:** Explore Tromsø Museum, where you can delve into local Sami culture and history. A great introduction to the region's indigenous people.
- **Evening:** Go on a Northern Lights tour. Local guides will take you to the best spots for seeing this natural wonder. Dress warmly and prepare to be mesmerized by the celestial display.

Day 3: Fjord Tour and Dog Sledding

- **Morning:** Take a Fjord tour by boat or bus, offering breathtaking views of Tromsø's stunning landscapes. The journey along the fjords is peaceful, with opportunities for spotting wildlife.
- **Afternoon:** Experience the thrill of dog sledding. Mush your own team of huskies through the Arctic wilderness or ride with an experienced guide.
- **Evening:** Relax at Huken Pub, a cozy spot in the city center known for its rustic charm and local beers.

Day 4: Sami Culture and Reindeer Sledding

- **Morning:** Head to a Sami Camp to learn about Sami culture. The Sami are Norway's indigenous people, and this experience offers a unique cultural insight. Enjoy a traditional Sami meal in a Lavvu (Sami tent).
- **Afternoon:** Try reindeer sledding, an ancient Sami tradition. The serene, snowy landscape creates a peaceful atmosphere, unlike any other outdoor activity.
- **Evening:** Take a break and have dinner at Mathallen, where you can savor creative Nordic cuisine in a modern, upscale setting.

Day 5: Snowmobiling and Tromsø Cable Car

- **Morning:** Gear up for an adrenaline-filled morning of snowmobiling. You'll zoom through pristine snow-covered valleys and

across frozen lakes while soaking in the untouched Arctic beauty.
- **Afternoon:** Take the Tromsø Cable Car up to Mount Storsteinen. At the top, you'll enjoy panoramic views of the city, fjords, and surrounding mountains. If you're feeling adventurous, hike around for a closer look at the Arctic wilderness.
- **Evening:** Have a relaxed dinner at Bardus Bistro. They offer local dishes like reindeer stew, in a relaxed, casual setting.

Day 6: Whale Watching and Arctic-Alpine Botanic Garden

- **Morning:** Embark on a whale-watching excursion. From November to January, humpback and killer whales can be spotted in the fjords around Tromsø. This is an unforgettable experience.

- **Afternoon:** Visit the Arctic-Alpine Botanic Garden, the world's northernmost botanic garden. It's especially beautiful in the summer, showcasing Arctic plants and rare species.
- **Evening:** Take it easy with dinner at Skirri by the harbor. Enjoy the calm ambiance with fresh seafood and picturesque views of the fjord.

Day 7: Shopping and Souvenirs

- **Morning:** Spend the morning browsing Storgata, Tromsø's main shopping street. Pick up unique souvenirs, from Sami handicrafts to Arctic-inspired artwork.
- **Afternoon:** Visit the Jekta Storsenter, Tromsø's largest shopping center. It's perfect for last-minute gifts or a cozy coffee break before you leave.

- **Evening:** End your trip with a farewell dinner at Emma's Dream Kitchen, a highly recommended restaurant offering authentic Norwegian dishes in an elegant setting.

30 phrases in Tromsø

1. Hei! – Hello!
2. God morgen! – Good morning!
3. God ettermiddag! – Good afternoon!
4. God kveld! – Good evening!
5. Ha det bra! – Goodbye!
6. Vennligst. – Please.
7. Takk. – Thank you.
8. Vær så snill. – Please (formal).
9. Unnskyld. – Excuse me.
10. Beklager. – Sorry.
11. Hvordan har du det? – How are you?
12. Jeg har det bra. – I'm doing well.

13. Hvor er busstasjonen? – Where is the bus station?

14. Hvor lang tid tar det å gå dit? – How long does it take to walk there?

15. Hvor mye koster en billett til...? – How much is a ticket to...?

16. Er det ledige drosjer i nærheten? – Are there taxis available nearby?

17. Når går neste ferge til...? – When is the next ferry to...?

18. Kan jeg få menyen, takk? – Can I get the menu, please?

19. Har dere noen vegetarretter? – Do you have any vegetarian dishes?

20. Jeg er allergisk mot nøtter. – I'm allergic to nuts.

21. Kan jeg få regningen, takk? – Can I have the bill, please?

22. Hva anbefaler du? – What do you recommend?

23. Er dette tradisjonell norsk mat? – Is this traditional Norwegian food?

24. Hvor mye koster dette? – How much does this cost?

25. Har dere noen lokale suvenirer? – Do you have any local souvenirs?

26. Kan jeg betale med kort? – Can I pay by card?

27. Finnes det noen håndlagde varer her? – Are there any handmade goods here?

28. Jeg ser etter en gave. – I'm looking for a gift.

29. Kan du hjelpe meg? – Can you help me?

30. Hvor er nærmeste apotek? – Where is the nearest pharmacy?

Conclusion

To wrap up your journey through the wonders of Tromsø, it's clear that this Arctic gem has so much to offer for travelers seeking adventure, cultural immersion, and breathtaking natural beauty. Whether you're planning to stay at one of the luxurious hotels like the Radisson Blu or prefer the cozy charm of a midrange option, Tromsø's accommodations are as diverse as its attractions. The experiences here are vast, from watching the magical Northern Lights dance across the sky to feeling the thrill of dog sledding across snowy landscapes, each moment in Tromsø is filled with excitement and wonder.

Exploring the local culture offers its own rewards, whether it's through the distinct flavors of Tromsø's cuisine, discovering the art and history in places like the Arctic Cathedral and Polaria Aquarium, or connecting with the Sami culture through reindeer sledding. You'll not only learn but also feel a deeper connection to the land and its people. The warmth of Tromsø's community comes through in every interaction, be it at the local markets, boutique stores, or even in the helpful hands of hotel staff. Every detail makes Tromsø a place of both great natural beauty and human connection. As you explore Tromsø's outdoor activities like snowmobiling or trekking the Arctic wilderness, the adventure never stops. You'll feel the thrill of conquering new terrain, the awe of nature's grandeur, and the peaceful stillness that can only be found in such a remote location. The practical information, booking tips, and useful local phrases help prepare you for a smooth and enriching experience in this remarkable city.

Whether you're a solo adventurer, a couple looking for a romantic getaway, or a family hoping to create lasting memories, Tromsø promises a lifetime of stories to tell. With its mixture of stunning landscapes, vibrant culture, and unique activities, Tromsø stands out as one of the world's most captivating destinations. Each day spent here feels like a new chapter in your own personal adventure, filled with excitement, discovery, and a deep sense of connection to the Arctic world.

Printed in Great Britain
by Amazon